photography by Martin Brigdale

Quadrille
PUBLISHING

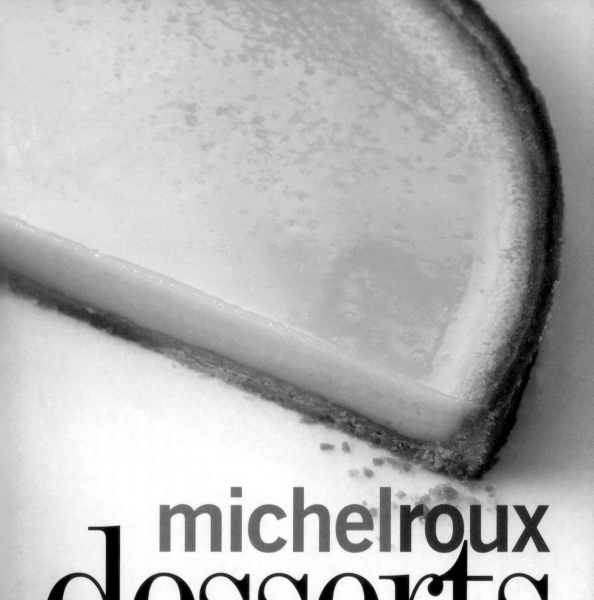

michelroux
desserts

notes

All spoon measures are level unless otherwise stated: 1tsp = 5ml spoon; 1tbsp = 15ml spoon.

Egg sizes are given where they are critical, otherwise use medium eggs, preferably organic or free-range. Anyone who is pregnant or in a vulnerable health group should avoid sauces that use raw egg whites or lightly cooked eggs.

Use fresh herbs, sea salt and freshly ground black pepper unless otherwise suggested.

If using the zest of citrus fruit, buy organic, unwaxed fruit.

Timings are for fan-assisted ovens. If using a conventional oven, increase the temperature by 15°C (1 Gas mark). Use an oven thermometer to check the temperature.

Editorial director **Anne Furniss**
Creative director **Mary Evans**
Project editor **Janet Illsley**
Translator **Sally Somers**
Photographer **Martin Brigdale**
Production **Leonie Kellman**

First published in 2011 by
Quadrille Publishing Limited
Alhambra House
27-31 Charing Cross Road
London WC2H 0LS
www.quadrille.co.uk

Text © 2011 Michel Roux
Photography © 2011 Martin Brigdale
Design and layout © 2011 Quadrille Publishing Limited

Cataloguing in Publication Data: a catalogue record for this book is available from the British Library.

ISBN 978 184400 983 1

Printed in China

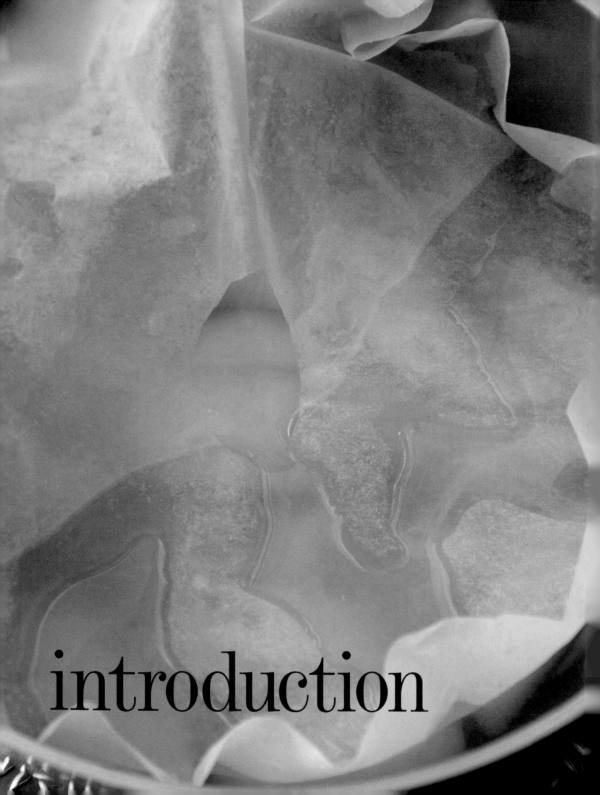

introduction

Over the past couple of decades, the creative development of desserts has been astounding. The handful of leading experts in this field took some time to realise that their *raison d'être* was out of step with the rest of the culinary world. But things have changed… so much for the better.

As far as my own cooking is concerned, I have always been keen to innovate. One of my favourite creations at the Waterside Inn is our inimitable 'Péché Gourmand' (sin on a plate), comprising a throng of mini desserts that change according to the season, and which has featured on the menu for more than twenty years. Simplicity is optimised and style minimised, reinforcing the concept of less is more.

Desserts should never be considered the poor cousin of the culinary world, and I intend to demonstrate that the reverse is true, offering in this book a marvellous assortment of desserts, from simple and light to the most seductively luxuriant.

Fruit plays the starring role, with sugar, cream and butter used in moderation. I make use of various herbs and aromatics – rosemary, thyme, bay, basil, lavender etc. – and spices – nutmeg, star anise, cloves, ginger and cinnamon – to emphasise or prolong the flavours. Just as for general cooking, I keep my pepper pot handy at all times, frequently applying a few turns over melon, papaya, and even strawberries – effective and much healthier than adding sugar.

I have not turned my back on my classic recipes, but developed and modernised them wherever I have found advantages in doing so. I have created new harmonies as well as combinations of colours, flavours and textures, just as I do in my general cooking.

The sublime quality of the photographs in this book – taken by my friend, artist-photographer Martin Brigdale – allows every dessert to be seen and enjoyed in all its splendour, and should inspire total confidence when it comes to following the recipes.

Eggs I always use free-range, organic eggs, if possible from small producers where the hens are kept outdoors all the time. Eggs that you buy from supermarkets are individually date-stamped; always use very fresh eggs, well within the date. If you've bought direct from a farm, keep the eggs in their original packaging marked with the date of laying. I use medium eggs in my recipes, weighing between 55 and 60g. Take eggs out of the fridge an hour or so before using, to bring them to room temperature. Many desserts use raw or lightly cooked eggs; it is essential that *very* fresh eggs are used for these recipes.

Butter Unsalted butter is my preferred choice for cooking. A 'dry' butter, meaning one with a maximum water content of 16%, will give the best results. Taste a little of your raw butter from time to time, to make sure it has a clean flavour with no hint of rancidity. If you keep an opened packet of butter in the fridge for several days, its qualities will diminish, particularly its taste.

Flour I like to use a good-quality organic flour. Mostly I use French white flour Type 45, which is finer and whiter than Type 55, and is ideal for all desserts. It is available from specialist suppliers (and online). As humidity is the enemy of flour, it should be kept in a dry place, preferably in an airtight container.

Sugar I mostly use caster sugar in my desserts, although icing sugar and demerara also feature: both are used to caramelise the surface of crème brûlées, for example. Once a packet of sugar has been opened, it's advisable to transfer the contents to an airtight container to avoid crystallisation; sugar doesn't like moisture. I use only as much sugar as a recipe really needs; overly sweet desserts are unhealthy and never taste as good.

Gelatine Different brands of gelatine vary in their setting capacity. I only ever use and recommend bronze leaf gelatine, each leaf or 'sheet' weighing 4g. It's important not to use more than the stated amount of gelatine, to ensure you achieve a soft, melting quality. Leaf gelatine needs to be soaked before use to soften: simply place in a shallow dish containing enough cold water to cover and leave for 5 minutes or so, then remove and squeeze out the excess water (shown right) before stirring into a mixture, which must be hot to ensure the gelatine dissolves.

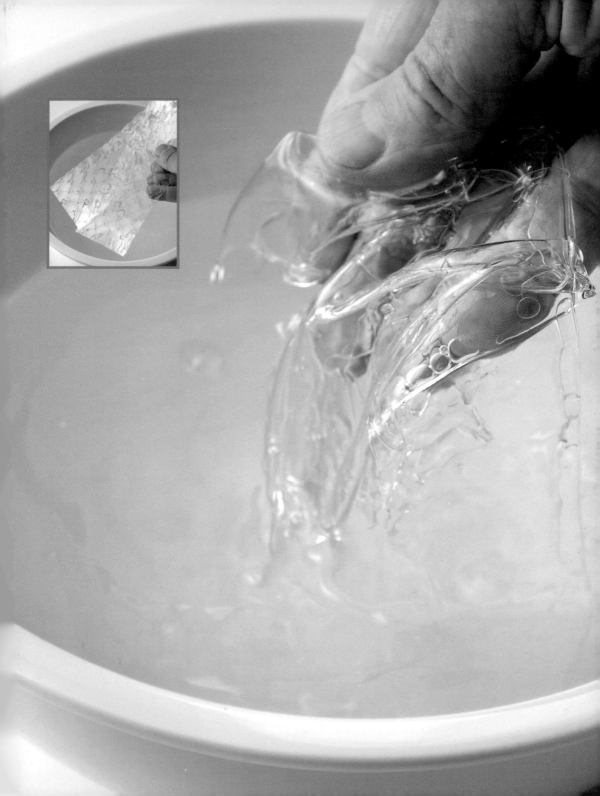

Chocolate I always use good-quality dark chocolate (usually Valrhona) with at least 70% cocoa solids, or couverture with a maximum of 76% cocoa solids. If the percentage is any higher than this I find it unpleasantly bitter to taste. You can buy couverture in block form, bars or chips. Chocolate or couverture is best melted in a bain-marie (or a heatproof bowl set over a pan of barely simmering water, making sure the bowl isn't touching the water). You need to check that the couverture or chocolate doesn't go any higher than 50–55°C and that you use it melted only once it has cooled to between 28 and 32°C. Couverture is used for dipping and decorating, as well as for ganache and all kinds of chocolate desserts.

Liquid glucose This is a pure carbohydrate, made in part from cornstarch or potato flour. It has a fairly viscous consistency and, unlike sugar, it won't crystallise. I use it when making stock syrup (page 275) and Italian meringue (page 152). It stabilises and improves texture, and is therefore generally loved by pâtissiers.

Lemon For me, this is the king of all ingredients. Lemon juice brings flavours to life, prevents the oxidation of fruits such as peaches, pears etc., and is incredibly versatile. It is also bursting with vitamin C. For flavouring and decoration, I frequently use the grated zest and peel of the fruit – as it is or candied. To get the maximum amount of juice from a lemon, heat it in a microwave for 20 seconds, then roll on your work surface before halving and squeezing. If you are using the zest or peel, it is important to buy unwaxed or organic fruit.

Herbs and spices Herbs and fresh aromatics, such as mint, rosemary, basil, tarragon, coriander, flat-leaf parsley, bay, lavender and lemongrass, can enhance fruit-based desserts significantly, helping the fruit to assert its character. Similarly, spices, such as star anise, vanilla, nutmeg, freshly ground pepper, cloves, quatre-épices, cayenne pepper, cinnamon and ginger, can be used sparingly to lend an enticing warmth and aroma.

Stevia is a herb with extraordinary potential: there are over 150 species and they all contain natural sweeteners. This new 'sugar' has a sweetening strength 200 times greater than sugar, and most significantly has no calories whatsoever. It can be found commercially in some parts of Europe, particularly Switzerland, but occasionally also in plant form. If you happen to come across the herb in a garden centre, I urge you to buy one. Pick and use the leaves as needed – just 2 or 3 is enough to sweeten a fruit salad for 8 people.

Measuring tools For successful desserts, ingredients must be weighed accurately, so you will need a good set of weighing scales or electronic digital scales, plus a set of measuring spoons and a measuring jug. You will also require a cook's thermometer to check the temperature of sauces, such as sabayons.

Pots and pans A high-quality set of durable pans is a worthwhile investment, as they will last a lifetime. I use All-clad pans, which give excellent results. A good non-stick frying pan is essential for making crêpes.

Knives A good-quality set of knives and an efficient sharpener is another asset. I recommend Global knives. For smoothing mixtures and transferring biscuits, meringues etc., a palette knife is indispensable.

Small electric appliances A free-standing mixer takes the effort out of strenuous whisking tasks – meringues, whisked sponges etc. – and a free-standing electric blender is useful for puréeing coulis and sauces. A hand-held stick blender is convenient too. For successful ice creams and sorbets, you will need an ice-cream maker.

Whisks, spatulas and spoons A classic long-handled metal balloon whisk with an easy-to-grip handle is used for whisking eggs, soufflés, sauces etc. A hand-held electric whisk is a labour-saving option, although I prefer to use a hand whisk for most tasks. You will also need a wooden spatula and a long-handled wooden spoon for stirring mixtures over heat, and a rubber spatula for folding aerated mixtures together.

Strainers and sieves For straining, a conical strainer made of perforated metal, known as a chinois, is useful. A conical wire-meshed sieve, known as a chinois fin, is useful for fine straining tasks. For most dry sifting purposes, however, you will need a fine-meshed, round sieve.

Tins and moulds A few baking trays, a selection of flan rings and/or loose-based flan tins (20cm, 22cm and 23cm), a couple of loose-based and/or springform cake tins (20cm and 23cm) and a selection of individual metal rings (5–8cm) will cover most requirements. One or two loaf tins and a set of dariole moulds will also be useful.

Other items You'll also need a zester, a grater such as a Microplane, a ladle, a large metal spoon, a skimming spoon, pastry brushes, a cook's blowtorch, an ice-cream scoop, Pyrex mixing bowls of various sizes, a pie dish, baking dishes, ramekins, gratin dishes, a 1 litre pudding basin and a selection of soufflé dishes.

Segments of citrus fruit, such as oranges and pink grapefruit, make a lovely simple decoration for all manner of desserts and they are easy to prepare.

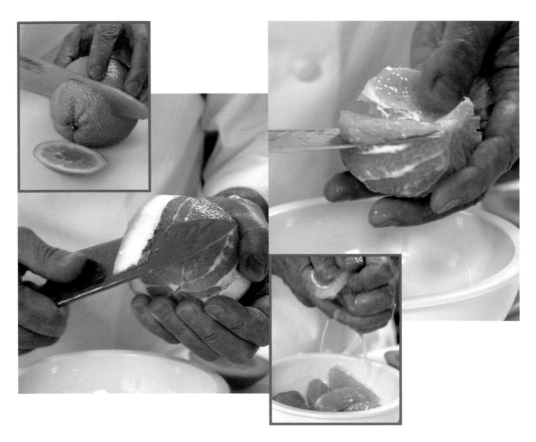

Using a sharp knife, slice off the top and bottom of the citrus fruit. Holding the fruit over a bowl to catch any juice, cut away the peel in thick slices, following the contour of the fruit and removing the pith as well. Cut down both sides of each segment to release it from the membrane and allow it to drop into the bowl. Once all the segments are removed, squeeze the membrane to extract all juice.

oven-drying fruit slices

Fine slices of fruit – such as pineapple, apple and pear – can be oven-dried until crisp and translucent to make delicate decorations for desserts and are prepared in a similar way. Blackberries and raspberries can also be oven-dried: quarter the berries and dry in the oven on its lowest setting for 6 hours. Crush the dried berries before sprinkling onto mousses etc.

To prepare pineapple, cut off the top and bottom, then stand upright and slice off the outer skin. Now prise out the 'eyes' with the tip of a knife. Turn the fruit on its side and carefully slice across into very thin rounds, using a very sharp knife. Lay the slices on a baking sheet lined with baking parchment and sprinkle with an even layer of icing sugar. Place in the oven at 90°C/Gas ¼ for 2–3 hours until the pineapple slices are dry and crisp with an intense pineapple aroma.

Whatever the season, there will always be fruit, tempting us with its assortment of colours, shapes and fragrances. I love using fruit in my desserts – either raw in its natural state, or poached, baked or grilled. It's just bursting with vitamins and goodness, and you can never eat too much of it. Before using fruit in a recipe, I urge you to first taste it raw. If it is in a perfect state of ripeness, it will be juicy, delicious and above all very sweet, which means you can cut down a little on the amount of sugar called for in your chosen recipe.

fruit desserts

redcurrant coulis

350g de-stalked redcurrants
juice of 1 lemon
100ml stock syrup (page 275)

Strain through a muslin-lined sieve (or a fine-meshed conical sieve) into a bowl. When most of the juice has strained through, gather two corners of the muslin in each hand and twist in opposite directions to extract the remaining juice.

Tip the redcurrants into a blender or food processor. Add the lemon juice and stock syrup and whiz for about 1 minute to a purée.

A soft fruit coulis is delicious served with poached pale-fleshed fruits like peaches and pears, or with vanilla ice cream or an iced soufflé.

blackberry coulis Put 350g hulled ripe blackberries, 50ml kirsch, 150ml stock syrup (page 275) and the juice of $1/2$ lemon in a blender and whiz for about 1 minute until puréed. Strain through a muslin-lined sieve or fine-meshed conical sieve into a bowl. Serves 8

blackcurrant coulis Put 450g de-stalked blackcurrants in a blender with 150ml stock syrup (page 275) and the juice of 1 lemon. Process until smooth, then strain through a muslin-lined or fine-meshed sieve into a bowl. Taste for sweetness and add extra sugar if necessary. Serves 6

raspberry coulis Put 500g hulled very ripe raspberries in a blender with 100ml stock syrup (page 275) and the juice of $1/2$ lemon. Whiz for 1 minute, then pass the coulis through a muslin-lined or fine-meshed conical sieve. Serves 8

makes about 600ml

500g apples (ideally Granny Smith)
75g caster sugar
½ lemon, washed and cut into 6 pieces
1 rosemary sprig

Cut each apple into 6 wedges and remove the core and pips, but do not peel. Put the apple pieces into a saucepan with 375ml water, the sugar, lemon and rosemary. Cover and cook over a gentle heat until the mixture is almost the consistency of a purée.

Discard the rosemary sprig, then transfer the mixture to a food processor or blender and process for 1½ minutes, until it is the smooth texture of a coulis. Strain through a fine sieve or chinois into a bowl and leave to cool.

Once cold, store in a sealed container in the fridge for up to a week, unless serving straight away.

This coulis is an ideal partner for a variety of desserts, including meringues, crêpes and lemon cake.

fruit salad with exotic fruit ice cubes

serves 6

Exotic fruit ice cubes bring extra flavour and an original touch to a fresh fruit salad, especially if you make the ice cubes in novelty-shaped moulds (as shown).

200g each of 6 ripe seasonal fruit, such as assorted summer berries, cherries and peaches; or pineapple, bananas, mango, kiwi fruit, grapes and pears in autumn/winter

ice cubes
1 ripe mango
50g caster sugar
6 ripe kiwi fruit
100ml pomegranate juice (fresh from a carton)

First make the ice cubes. Using a knife, peel the mango and cut the flesh from the stone. Put into a food processor or blender with 50ml water and the caster sugar and process for 1 minute. Pour this pulp into an ice-cube tray and put into the freezer.

Using a knife, peel the skin from the kiwi fruit, then cut the flesh into pieces and purée in the (cleaned) food processor or blender for 30 seconds. Pass through a fine sieve set over a jug, pressing the fruit down with the back of a ladle to extract as much juice as possible. Pour into another ice-cube tray and transfer to the freezer. Pour the pomegranate juice into another ice-cube tray and place in the freezer.

To make the fruit salad, wash each fruit and hull or peel and prepare as necessary, according to the type of fruit. Halve, cut into slices or leave whole, depending on size.

To serve, combine the prepared fruits in a large, shallow dish, un-mould the ice cube shapes and arrange these randomly over the fruit salad. Serve immediately.

You could sweeten the fruit salad by snipping over a few leaves of stevia – an unusual and delicious herb, which lends sweetness without sugar.

serves 4

This simple dessert can be prepared in advance – ready to add the honey glaze at the last moment, for an appealing sheen.

6 tbsp runny honey
4 star anise
6 white or yellow peaches
juice of 2 lemons
small pinch of freshly grated nutmeg

Preheat the oven to 180°C/Gas 4. Bring a medium saucepan of water to the boil. Put the honey and star anise into a small pan and heat gently for 5 minutes.

Meanwhile, skin the peaches. Have ready a bowl of iced water. Using the point of a knife, make a shallow incision around the middle of each peach. Using a slotted spoon, drop the peaches gently into the boiling water. As soon as the skin lifts off at the incision point, remove the peaches with the slotted spoon and immerse in the iced water. Peel away the skin from each peach with the point of the knife.

Place 4 peaches in a small roasting dish and spoon the honey over them. Roast in the oven for 8–10 minutes, depending on the ripeness of the peaches, basting every 2 or 3 minutes with the honey. Transfer the peaches to a plate with the star anise and set aside to cool.

Pour two-thirds of the lemon juice into the honey in the roasting dish and place over a gentle heat. Simmer gently to reduce until the glaze coats the back of a spoon. Set aside.

Halve and stone the other 2 peeled peaches. Put into a food processor or blender with the remaining lemon juice and the nutmeg, and process to a smooth coulis.

To serve, divide the coulis between 4 wide serving glasses. Place a roasted peach in each glass, then coat with the almost-cooled honey and top each with a star anise.

serves 8

I adore this sensual dessert: the spices add an extra dimension to the juicy pineapple flavours. It is particularly good served with a scoop of thyme-scented fromage frais sorbet (page 137).

1 ripe pineapple, about 1.8kg
16 cloves
50ml grapeseed or groundnut oil

syrup
400g light brown sugar
100g caster sugar
16 dried Sichuan peppercorns, crushed
4g quatre épices (a mixture of pepper,
   cloves, nutmeg and ginger)
6 star anise

For the syrup, put 1 litre water into a saucepan and add all the ingredients. Slowly bring to the boil over a gentle heat, stirring occasionally. Now simmer over a medium heat to reduce by three-quarters, to make a thick syrup. Set aside.

Preheat the oven to 180°C/Gas 4. Using a serrated knife, cut a 3cm slice from the top of the pineapple, removing the leafy fronds, and a 2cm slice from the base to enable the pineapple to stand upright. Now working from top to bottom and following the curve of the fruit, remove the peel. To remove the little black 'eyes', and create an attractive finish at the same time, cut a spiral groove, 5mm deep, around the entire fruit. Stud the flesh evenly all over with the cloves.

Heat the oil in an oval pan (or one that will take the whole fruit) until very hot, then add the pineapple and lightly colour all over. Transfer the pineapple to a medium-small roasting dish, standing it upright. Baste the pineapple with the reduced syrup and roast in the oven for 35–40 minutes, depending on the ripeness of the fruit, basting it every 5 minutes or so with the syrup, and keeping it upright.

Leave the roasted pineapple to stand for 10–15 minutes before serving, basting from time to time with the syrup.

To serve, lie the
pineapple on its side
and cut into slices,
about 1cm thick.
Arrange in a serving
dish, retaining
the star anise for
decoration, and
serve just warm.

poached pears stuffed with dates and figs

serves 6

Simple to prepare and delectable to eat – owing to the harmonious combination of flavours – this is an autumn and winter dessert *par excellence*.

6 perfectly ripe pears, ideally William or Conference
juice of 1 lemon
400g caster sugar
1 cinnamon stick, broken into pieces
200g dates, stoned
100g soft dried figs
1½ tbsp rum (optional)
400ml caramel sauce (page 275), to serve

Using a small, very sharp knife, mark a decorative scalloped-shaped collar in the skin around the top of each pear, then peel away the skin from the collar to the base of the pear. Using a melon baller and working through the base, scoop out the core and pips.

Stand the pears upright in a saucepan just large enough to hold them snugly. Pour in 1 litre water and add the lemon juice, sugar and cinnamon stick. Slowly bring to the boil over a gentle heat and poach the pears at a light simmer for 10–15 minutes, depending on their ripeness. Transfer the poached pears and their syrup to a dish and set aside to cool completely.

Finely dice the dates and figs and combine in a bowl. Pour on the rum (or 1½ tbsp water) and mix together lightly using your fingertips.

When ready to serve, carefully drain the pears. Using a teaspoon, fill the cavity of each pear generously with the date and fig mixture, from the base. Place each pear on an individual serving plate and pour the caramel sauce around. Any excess stuffing can be spooned alongside the fruit.

These delicate fruit-filled baskets are best cooked shortly before serving and filled at the last moment. As they are fragile, it's a good idea to make a few extra to allow for breakages.

brandy snap baskets
100g butter, melted
100g caster sugar
100g golden syrup
100g plain flour
40g fresh root ginger, peeled and grated
juice of ½ lemon
1 tbsp Cognac

filling
2 young, tender rhubarb stalks
500ml stock syrup (page 275)
juice of 1 orange
250g crème chantilly (page 272)
18 perfectly ripe raspberries

For the filling, peel the rhubarb if necessary, wash in cold water, then cut into batons about 3cm long and 5mm across. Bring the stock syrup to the boil in a pan. Add the rhubarb and poach for 20 seconds, then tip the rhubarb and syrup into a dish and set aside. Simmer the orange juice in a pan to reduce by half; leave to cool.

To make the brandy snap baskets, preheat the oven to 180°C/Gas 4. Mix the butter, sugar and golden syrup together in a bowl, using a wooden spoon. Add the flour, ginger, lemon juice and Cognac, and whisk until smooth. Using a shallow 15cm ring, shape at least 6 rounds on a lightly buttered baking tray, spacing them 5cm apart to allow room for spreading: fill the ring to a 3–4cm depth with a little of the mixture, smooth with a spatula, then lift off the ring and repeat. Cook in the oven for 3–5 minutes, until they turn a light caramel colour.

Leave the brandy snap rounds on the tray for 30 seconds–1 minute. Then, using a palette knife, lift one and place in an individual tartlet tin, small bowl or large cup, about 6cm in diameter and 3.5cm high. Shape into baskets by gently pressing the brandy snap into the mould and fluting the edges. Repeat to shape the rest. Leave until cold, then carefully de-mould and place on a wire rack.

Fold the orange juice into the crème chantilly and divide between the brandy snap baskets. Arrange the raspberries and drained rhubarb on top. Serve immediately.

curd cheese with berries and passion fruit

serves 4

A lovely, light dessert, that makes a perfect brunch dish, too. For the simple flavours to really shine through, it's important that the cheese isn't too cold when you assemble this dessert.

300g ripe red berries in season (blackberries,
  small strawberries, raspberries, redcurrants etc.)
1½ tbsp grapeseed oil
30g caster sugar
10g flat-leaf parsley, finely snipped
2 passion fruit
300g ricotta or other curd cheese, at room temperature
freshly ground black pepper

Carefully wash the berries, drain and hull or de-stalk them. Heat the oil in a non-stick pan over a medium heat. Add the blackberries and cook for 1 minute, then add the strawberries, raspberries, redcurrants and any other more delicate berries you are using. After another minute, add the sugar and parsley and cook for 30 seconds. Immediately tip the fruits with their juices into a sieve set over a bowl to drain, reserving the juice. Transfer the drained fruits to another bowl and set aside.

Pour the juice back into the pan and simmer to reduce by half, then return to the empty bowl. Cut the passion fruit in half, scoop out the pulp and seeds with a spoon and add to the reduced juice. Stir to combine.

Set a ring, about 9cm in diameter and 3cm high, on an individual deep plate. Lightly season the curd cheese with a little freshly ground black pepper. Put a tablespoonful of curd cheese inside the ring, without packing it down. Add a quarter of the berries and top with another tablespoonful of curd cheese, spreading in gently but still without pressing it down. Remove the ring and pour a quarter of the passion fruit and reduced juice mixture over the top.

Repeat to assemble the other three desserts. Serve at once.

serves 4

You can vary the tropical fruits for this healthy dessert, but you do need to use varieties with a fairly firm flesh that won't fall apart on cooking. For a special touch, serve with a kirsch sabayon (page 69).

1 ripe dwarf pineapple, about 700g
1 papaya (not too ripe), about 600g
4 dwarf bananas (not too ripe)
5g black peppercorns, finely crushed
3g pure ground vanilla (3 generous knife tips)
4 small limes
2 tbsp grapeseed oil
1 tbsp runny honey
2 passion fruit

Using a serrated knife, cut off the leafy fronds from the pineapple, then remove the skin. Split the pineapple in half lengthways, remove the core, then cut the flesh into roughly 2cm pieces. Set aside in a shallow dish.

Halve the papaya lengthways, scoop out the seeds, then remove the skin. Cut the flesh into roughly 2cm pieces and add to the pineapple pieces. Peel the bananas, cut into 2cm lengths and set aside with the other prepared fruits.

Mix the crushed pepper and vanilla together, sprinkle over the fruits and mix gently. Now spear the pieces of fruit, alternating them as you do so, onto 4 long or 8 short metal skewers. Halve the limes, or quarter if using 8 skewers, then spear a piece onto the end of each skewer, flesh-side next to the fruit; this will hold the fruit in place.

Preheat a flat griddle pan or heat up the barbecue. Mix the oil and honey together in a small bowl and use a brush to lightly dab the fruits with the mixture. Transfer the brochettes to the griddle or barbecue when it is ready. Cook, turning frequently so they colour evenly, for about 3 minutes, until lightly marked.

Place the brochettes on individual serving plates. Halve the passion fruit and scoop out the pulp and seeds over the brochettes. The lime on the end of each skewer can be squeezed over the fruits as you serve them.

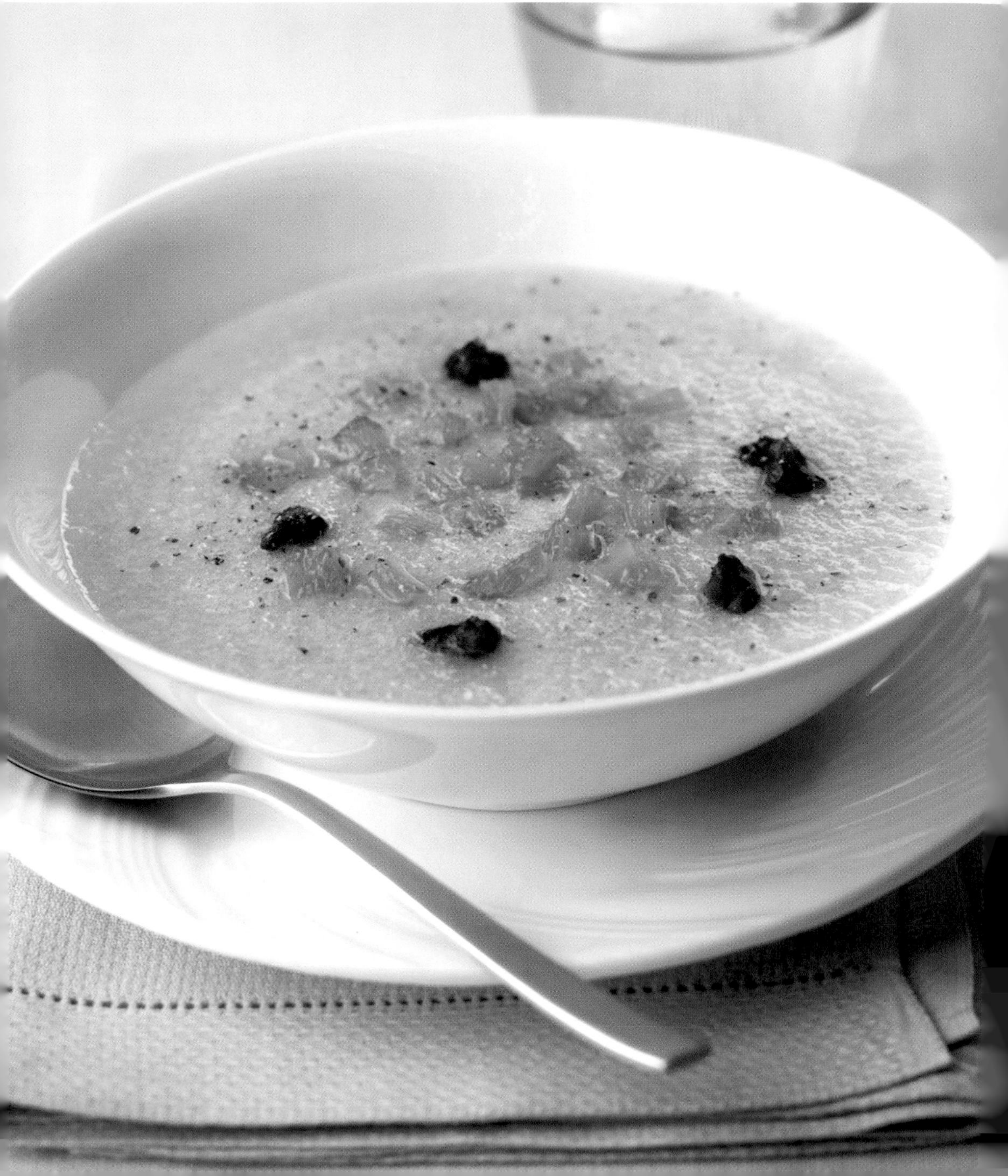

serves 4

Prepared in just a few minutes, and wonderfully refreshing, this is
a perfect summer dessert.

1 melon, preferably Galia, about 800g
2 green peppers, about 180g each
4 tbsp caster sugar
freshly ground white (or black) pepper
6 ripe raspberries

Using a knife, pare off the melon skin, removing a thickness of about 5mm. Halve the melon and remove the seeds. Cut the melon flesh into large cubes.

Split the peppers in half and remove the white pith and seeds. Cut into large strips and, using a potato peeler, peel away the skin. Cut a quarter of the pepper into fine julienne and slice across into tiny cubes, then put into a saucepan with the sugar. Add enough cold water just to cover and bring to the boil. Remove from the heat and set aside to cool; reserve for the garnish.

Put the melon cubes and pepper strips into a blender or food processor and process for 2 minutes. Season with 3 turns of the pepper mill, then strain through a chinois or sieve and refrigerate.

To serve, lightly whisk the chilled gazpacho, then divide between 4 deep bowls. Sprinkle the tiny sugared pepper cubes over the surface. Lightly crush the raspberries between your fingers and drop little bursts around the pepper cubes. Grind a little white pepper over the gazpacho and serve very cold.

pear 'minestrone' with chestnuts and cinnamon

serves 6

This simple and delicious combination is perfect for autumn.
I adore the contrast of the velvety smooth pear coulis and the
crunch of the chestnuts.

60g caster sugar
400g ripe pears
juice of 1 lemon
2 pinches of ground cinnamon
8 fresh chestnuts
20g icing sugar

Pour 700ml water into a saucepan, add the sugar and dissolve over a medium heat.
Peel the pears, cut in half and remove the stalks, cores and pips, then squeeze the
lemon juice over the halves. When the sugar syrup comes to the boil, add the pear
halves and poach over a gentle heat for 5–10 minutes, depending on ripeness.

Scoop out one pear half and reserve for the garnish. Put the rest of the poached
pear halves into a food processor or blender with a third of the syrup and a pinch
of cinnamon. Process for 1 minute, then strain the pear coulis through a fine sieve
or chinois into a bowl. Leave to cool, then cover and refrigerate.

To prepare the chestnuts, preheat the oven to 200°C/Gas 6. Using a small knife, slit
the chestnut skins to a depth of 5mm on one side only. Roast in the oven for about
10 minutes, turning halfway. The heat will split the skins open; the flesh will be firm
but cooked. Wrap the chestnuts in a tea towel for 2 minutes, then peel off the skins
and softer inner peel, using a small knife. Turn the oven up to 240°C/Gas 9. Break the
chestnuts into little pieces, put onto a small baking tray and sprinkle with the icing
sugar. Briefly place in the very hot oven to caramelise the sugar.

Divide the pear coulis between serving bowls. Dice the reserved pear half and scatter
over the surface, along with the chestnut pieces. Sprinkle with a pinch of cinnamon.
Serve cold, but not overly chilled.

autumn fruit crumble

serves 8

Quince and ginger lend a wonderful fragrance to this crumble.
You can vary the fruits according to the season – plums and blackberries are
a good combination. Serve with crème anglaise (page 56) or cream.

500ml stock syrup (page 275)
340g cranberries (fresh or frozen and defrosted)
4 quince
1 Bramley or other cooking apple
4 Cox or Gala apples
juice of 1 lemon
180g caster sugar
80g preserved stem ginger in syrup, cut into julienne

crumble
50g butter, cut into pieces, slightly softened
60g light brown sugar
100g plain flour

Bring the stock syrup to the boil in a pan. Drop in the cranberries, remove from the heat and set aside to soak for 2 hours, or until cold. Drain and set aside.

Preheat the oven to 190°C/Gas 5. Prick each quince in 3 or 4 places with a fork, wrap them all in a piece of foil and place on a baking tray. Bake for 1–1¼ hours until tender, turning 3 or 4 times during cooking. To test, insert a skewer into the flesh; it should go in easily. Unwrap all the quince and set aside to cool.

Meanwhile, peel, quarter and core all the apples, then cut the flesh into 2cm dice. Put into a saucepan with the lemon juice and caster sugar and cook over a high heat for 5 minutes, stirring often. Remove from the heat and set aside. Using a small knife, peel, halve and core the quince, then cut the flesh into 2cm dice.

To make the crumble, put the butter, brown sugar and flour into a bowl. Using your fingertips, rub together until the mixture reaches a grainy, almost sandy, but still slightly uneven consistency; do not overwork.

Gently mix the cranberries, quince and apples together in a pie dish (about 23x30cm). Scatter the ginger over the top, then press lightly into the fruit with your fingertips. Sprinkle the crumble topping evenly over the surface without packing it down. Bake at 190°C/Gas 5 for 40 minutes. Leave to stand for 5–10 minutes before serving.

serves 6

700g mixed soft fruits (ideally equal quantities
   of raspberries, strawberries, blackberries,
   blueberries and blackcurrants or redcurrants),
   plus 250g extra raspberries for the sauce
350g caster sugar
30g butter, melted, to grease
1 good-quality white sandwich loaf, cut into about
   14 medium slices

Wash the soft fruits carefully, except for the raspberries if they are already hulled, keeping the different fruits separate. Hull and de-stem strawberries and blackcurrants or redcurrants, as necessary.

In a medium saucepan, dissolve the sugar in 500ml water over a medium heat and slowly bring to the boil, then lower the heat. Every 20 seconds, immerse a different fruit into the sugar syrup in the following order: blackberries, strawberries, blackcurrants, blueberries, raspberries, redcurrants. Remove the pan from the heat 20 seconds after you add the last of the fruit. Cover the pan with cling film and set aside to allow the fruit to cool in the poaching liquid.

Meanwhile, purée the 250g raspberries in a blender and pass through a fine sieve. Once cold, carefully drain the poached fruit over a bowl to save the syrup. Mix one-third of the syrup into the raspberry purée.

Lightly brush the inside of a 900ml pudding basin with the melted butter. Trim the crusts from the bread slices. Cut an 8cm round from one slice; cut the remaining slices into strips, about 3cm wide.

illustrated on previous page

This classic is more familiar under the guise of summer pudding, but I am equally fond of serving it in the autumn, when berries are full flavoured and at their most fragrant. Vary the berries and fresh currants according to what is in season.

Dip the bread round into the raspberry syrup, then place in the bottom of the basin. One at a time, lightly dip the bread slices in the raspberry syrup, then arrange them, slightly overlapping, around the side of the basin to line it completely. Fill with the cooled, poached fruit and pour a little of the remaining raspberry syrup on top. (Save any leftover syrup to serve on the side, if you like.)

Top with a layer of bread strips, dunking them first in the raspberry syrup. Cover the pudding with cling film and put a plate that just fits inside the rim of the basin on top. Place a weight on top to help compress the pudding and refrigerate for 6–12 hours before serving.

When ready to serve, remove the weight, plate and cling film. Carefully slide a palette knife around the inside of the basin and turn out the pudding onto a shallow dish or lipped plate. You can either present it whole, or in individual portions, using a very sharp knife to cut it into wedges. Good, thick cream complements this slightly tart fruity dessert perfectly.

apple jelly

makes 650ml

250g caster sugar
500g apples (Cox or
    Gala), cored and
    cut into chunks
1 lemon, cut into
    chunks
6 sheets leaf gelatine

Pour 500ml water into a saucepan, add the sugar
and dissolve over a medium heat. Bring to the
boil and skim the surface, then add the apple
and lemon pieces. Lower the heat and simmer
for 10 minutes. Meanwhile, soften the gelatine in
a shallow dish of cold water for about 5 minutes.

Remove the pan from the heat. Use a spoon
to move aside the apple and lemon pieces and
create a space in the pan. Drain the gelatine
and squeeze out excess water.

Drop the gelatine leaves into the pan; they will
dissolve in the syrup. Using a ladle, transfer the
syrup and fruit to a muslin-lined chinois or sieve
set over a bowl or jug to catch the liquid. Allow it
to drip through slowly – do not press down on the
fruit or the jelly will be cloudy rather than clear.

I use the molten jelly as a coating for various cold desserts, such as bananas cooked in their skins (see overleaf) or fruit in a tart or tartlets. It can also be chilled to set, then chopped and served as part of a dessert. It has a lovely, subtle flavour and beautiful pale pink colour.

Once the liquid has drained through, it can be cooled and used as a glaze or coating. Or you can pour it into jars, set aside to cool, then refrigerate until set. It will keep well in the fridge for about 10 days and can be chopped to serve as part of a dessert.

baked bananas with apple jelly and blueberry compote

serves 4

Baking bananas whole in their skins produces a surprisingly good flavour and creamy texture. The jelly and blueberries add a delightful decorative touch to this otherwise straightforward dessert.

4 perfectly ripe medium bananas
juice of 1 lemon
50g caster sugar
200g blueberries
300ml set apple jelly (page 46)

Preheat the oven to 190°C/Gas 5. Lay the bananas on a baking tray and bake for 10 minutes, or until the skins are black, turning them over halfway. Set aside to cool for 15 minutes. Then, using a small, sharp knife, remove two-thirds of the banana skins, leaving only the underneath part intact. Brush the banana flesh lightly with the lemon juice to prevent it from discolouring. Leave to cool completely, then refrigerate.

Put 50ml water into a small saucepan, add the sugar and dissolve over a gentle heat, then slowly bring to the boil. Put the blueberries into a heatproof bowl and pour on the boiling syrup. Leave to cool, then drain the blueberries, reserving the syrup; refrigerate the berries. Return the syrup to the pan and simmer gently to reduce to a syrupy consistency. Remove from the heat and set aside.

Melt one-third of the apple jelly, then pour it into a dish set over a bowl of iced water and stir briefly every 2 minutes as it cools. As soon as the jelly starts to thicken slightly, use a brush to coat the banana flesh with it, then put back in the fridge. Cut the remaining jelly into dice and refrigerate.

To serve, lay a banana on each plate. Arrange a pile of jelly cubes alongside, make a well in the middle of them and fill with the blueberries. Spoon drops of the reduced blueberry syrup here and there over the jelly dice and serve.

citrus fruit in a sauternes jelly

serves 4

The success of this simple, delicate dish lies in choosing a good Sauternes wine and citrus fruits that are neither too sweet nor too sharp. Let the dessert speak for itself…

1 medium orange
½ grapefruit, ideally pink, cut vertically
1 lemon, washed
50g caster sugar
2 sheets leaf gelatine
375ml Sauternes, or best-quality sweet dessert wine

Using a very sharp, flexible-bladed knife, remove the peel and pith from the orange and grapefruit, to reveal the segments. Slide the knife blade between each one and the membranes to release the segments. Cut each orange segment into 4 pieces and each grapefruit segment into 6 pieces. Refrigerate the fruits in separate containers.

Using a potato peeler, pare the zest from the lemon, then cut into long, fine julienne. Put 50ml water and the sugar in a small pan, dissolve over a medium heat and bring to the boil. Reduce the heat, add the lemon zest and simmer gently for 6–8 minutes to candy. Drain off the syrup and lay the candied julienne out on baking parchment, so they don't stick together. Soften the gelatine in cold water to cover for 5 minutes.

In a small pan, warm 50ml Sauternes, then take off the heat. Drain the gelatine, squeeze out excess water and stir into the warm Sauternes to dissolve. Leave for 10 minutes, then stir into the rest of the Sauternes. Pour into a bowl, placed in a larger bowl of iced water to cool, giving a quick stir every 2–3 minutes. Drain the fruit well.

As soon as the wine starts to thicken slightly, pour it into chilled glasses. Working quickly, push the orange and grapefruit into the semi-set wine, using the point of a knife to sink the pieces to different depths, so they appear to be floating. Refrigerate for at least 2 hours. Decorate with the candied lemon zest to serve.

serves 8

These glorious lightly set jellies inspire romance. To enjoy them at their best,
use very ripe, flavourful fruit at the height of the season.

200g strawberries
200g raspberries
200g redcurrants
200g cherries
finely pared zest of 1 orange

100g caster sugar
4 sheets leaf gelatine
juice of 1 lemon
redcurrant sprigs or wild strawberries,
   to decorate

Wash each type of fruit separately, then hull the strawberries and raspberries if
necessary; strip the redcurrants off their stalks with the tines of a fork; stone and
halve the cherries. If the strawberries are large, halve them too.

Put all the fruits into a heatproof bowl with the orange zest, sugar and 150ml water.
Cover tightly with cling film and stand in a bain-marie or over a pan of barely
simmering water. Poach over a low heat (at 70–80°C) for about 40 minutes.

Meanwhile, soften the gelatine in a shallow dish of cold water for about 5 minutes.
Remove the bowl of fruit from the heat. Drain the gelatine, squeeze out excess water
and add to the hot fruit, stirring to dissolve. Re-cover and set aside to cool.

Strain the fruit through a muslin-lined sieve or chinois into a bowl. Add the lemon
juice to the liquid. Pour into small glasses and refrigerate for several hours until
lightly set.

Take the jellies out of the fridge about 20 minutes before serving to allow them
to soften at room temperature. Decorate each glass with a sprig of redcurrants
or wild strawberries.

Here is the grand spectacle of crèmes, with a colour palette ranging from pale pastel to dazzling bright, and textures that caress the palate, tempting you into pure indulgence. Many of these desserts come from other parts of the world, and I have fallen for them during my many travels to some sixty or so other countries. They form part of my repertoire and are close to my heart. I've also included sabayons, which are delectable eaten in their simplest form. They are silky-smooth both on the palate and to the eye, and take little time to prepare.

crèmes & sabayons

crème anglaise

makes about 750ml (6–8 servings)

The perfect accompaniment to so many desserts, this classic light, creamy custard can be flavoured to taste (see overleaf).

500ml milk
125g caster sugar
1 vanilla pod, split lengthways
6 egg yolks

Put the milk, two-thirds of the sugar and the vanilla pod into a heavy-based saucepan and slowly bring to the boil.

Meanwhile, whisk the egg yolks and remaining sugar together in a heatproof bowl. Continue to whisk until the mixture becomes pale and has a light ribbon consistency.

The custard will keep in a covered container in the fridge for up to 48 hours.

Cook over a low heat, stirring with a wooden spatula or spoon; do not let it boil or it may curdle. The custard is ready when it has thickened slightly – just enough to lightly coat the back of the spatula. When you run your finger through, it should leave a clear trace. Immediately take the pan off the heat.

Pour the boiling milk on to the egg yolks, whisking continuously, then pour the mixture back into the saucepan.

Unless you are serving the crème anglaise warm, pour through a fine sieve or chinois into a bowl set over crushed ice and leave to cool, stirring occasionally to prevent a skin from forming.

crème anglaise variations

chocolate crème anglaise Stir 60g melted good-quality bitter chocolate into the milk as you warm it. Makes about 750ml

coffee crème anglaise Stir 1 tbsp instant coffee powder into the hot milk. Makes about 750ml

ginger crème anglaise Infuse the milk with 20g peeled and finely sliced fresh root ginger rather than vanilla. Makes about 750ml

spiced crème anglaise Infuse the milk with 4 or 5 star anise instead of vanilla. Makes about 750ml

minted crème anglaise Infuse the milk with a bunch of fresh mint rather than vanilla. The freshness of this mint-flavoured custard goes brilliantly with all berries. It is also excellent with chocolate ice cream and chocolate truffle cake. Makes about 750ml

pistachio crème anglaise Either use 40g pistachio paste or 200g skinned fresh pistachio nuts soaked in cold water for 24 hours, then drained and crushed to a paste using a pestle and mortar. Pour one-third of the hot crème anglaise onto the pistachio paste, stirring with a whisk, then stir into the rest of the hot custard. Whiz in a blender for about 3 minutes, until very smooth. Pass through a fine sieve or chinois into a bowl, cool over crushed ice and chill until ready to use. This unusual custard is superb with pears poached in Sauternes. Makes about 750ml

Ready in minutes, this is the simplest of desserts, as its name suggests.
I like to serve it with French meringues (page 146) – either whole on
the side or roughly crushed and scattered over the top.

400g ripe strawberries
100g caster sugar
1–2 tsp good-quality aged balsamic vinegar,
**   to taste**
400ml whipping cream

Hull the strawberries, place in a dish and scatter with the sugar. Crush the berries
lightly with a fork, sprinkle with the balsamic vinegar, toss to mix and leave to
macerate for 10 minutes, to allow the strawberries to absorb the vinegar.

In another bowl, whip the cream to a ribbon consistency, then gently fold into the
crushed strawberry mixture. Spoon the fruit fool into 6 serving glasses and refrigerate
for 20 minutes or so before serving.

You can also make this with an apple, rhubarb or apricot compote,
replacing the macerated strawberries with an equal quantity of cooled
compote, giving you a fruit fool for every season.

chestnut creams with caramel sauce

serves 4

This exquisite dessert takes a little time to prepare,
but it is a real treat – for the eyes as well as the taste buds.

½ sheet leaf gelatine
180g tinned sweet chestnut purée, chilled
200ml whipping cream, chilled
100ml Cognac or Armagnac
8 long, fine langues de chat, half-coated
 in chocolate (page 266)
½ quantity caramel sauce (page 275)

chestnuts (optional)
6 fresh chestnuts
125ml milk

Soften the gelatine in a shallow dish of cold water for about 5 minutes. Whip the
chestnut purée and cream together in a bowl to a ribbon consistency. Heat the
Cognac in a small pan, then remove from the heat. Drain the gelatine and squeeze
out excess water, then add to the Cognac, stirring to dissolve. Transfer to a bowl and,
using a whisk, work in a quarter of the chestnut and cream mixture until it is evenly
combined, then fold in the rest.

Divide the mixture between 4 moulds, about 7cm in diameter and 6cm tall (ideally
decorative). Refrigerate for 4 hours.

For the chestnuts, if using, split the skin of each chestnut on one side to a depth of
5mm, using a small knife. Put into a small saucepan with the milk and 125ml water
and cook over a medium heat for 20–25 minutes. Remove from the heat and peel
off the skins and softer inner peel, using a small knife. Return the peeled chestnuts
to the pan and leave to cool in the milky liquid.

To turn out, dip the base of each mould in very hot water for 15 seconds, then invert
onto a serving plate. Drain the chestnuts thoroughly, if using, and press through a
small chinois or sieve, to create 'chestnut vermicelli'. Scatter on top of the creams.
Lay 2 langues de chat on each dessert and pour the caramel sauce around to serve.

chocolate and raspberry trifle

serves 6–8

In this trifle the layers are soft, so they intermingle delectably.

60g good-quality white chocolate, chopped
    into small pieces
150g chocolate Genoese (page 163), baked
    a day ahead
2 tbsp sweet dessert wine, preferably Maury
    or de Banyuls
200ml whipping cream
8 perfect raspberries
icing sugar, to dust

chocolate crème patissière
375ml milk
50g caster sugar
4 egg yolks
20g plain flour
20g dark, bitter cocoa powder

raspberry sauce
125g raspberries
juice of 1 lemon
60g icing sugar

For the crème patissière, heat the milk and two-thirds of the sugar in a pan. Whisk the egg yolks and remaining sugar in a bowl, using a balloon whisk, then whisk in the flour. As the milk boils, whisk in the cocoa, then pour onto the egg yolks, whisking all the time. Return to the pan, bring to the boil and let bubble for 30 seconds, still whisking. Pour into a dish, sprinkle lightly with icing sugar to prevent a skin forming and leave to cool, then cover with cling film and refrigerate (until chilled, but not set).

For the sauce, put the raspberries, lemon juice and icing sugar into a food processor or blender and blitz for 1 minute. Strain through a fine sieve and refrigerate.

Melt the white chocolate in a bain-marie or heatproof bowl set over a pan of water. Cut the Genoese sponge into 1.5cm cubes and place in the bottom of a large glass serving bowl, about 20cm in diameter and 7cm deep. Sprinkle the dessert wine evenly over, then cover with the crème patissière. Pour the raspberry sauce on top, then trickle the melted white chocolate over the surface.

Whip the cream to a ribbon consistency, then spoon on top of the trifle, peaking it with the end of a palette knife. Refrigerate for 2–3 hours.

To serve, arrange the raspberries on top and dust with a little icing sugar.

illustrated on previous page

serves 4

120g candied grapefruit peel strips (page 258)
4 dates
200g mascarpone
200ml whipping cream
200ml pistachio crème anglaise (page 58)

Cut the candied grapefruit peel strips into large dice. Quarter and stone the dates. Set aside 4 date quarters and a spoonful of the candied grapefruit for decoration. Dice the rest of the dates.

Put the mascarpone into a large bowl. In another bowl, whip the cream to a ribbon consistency, then fold into the mascarpone using a rubber spatula. Now fold in the diced dates and candied grapefruit, without overworking.

Using 2 large spoons dipped in hot water, shape a quenelle from the mascarpone mixture and place on an individual plate. Repeat for the other 3 servings. Decorate with the reserved date pieces and candied fruit. Pour a little pistachio crème anglaise around each quenelle and serve chilled.

This simple dessert takes only minutes to assemble. I like a few turns of the black pepper mill over the quenelles – it's a matter of individual taste, but I recommend you try it…

sabayon   **serves 4**

You will need a cook's thermometer to check the temperature of the sabayon.

100ml Sauternes or other sweet white wine
3 egg yolks
40g caster sugar

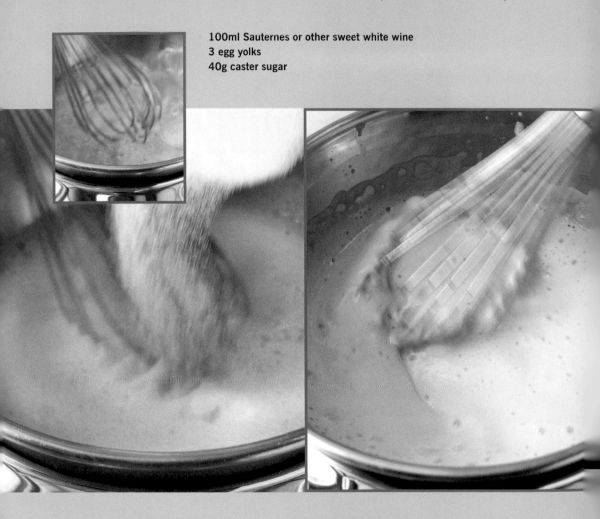

One-third fill a saucepan (large enough to hold the base of a heatproof, large round-bottomed bowl) with warm water, and heat gently. Pour the Sauternes into the bowl, then add the egg yolks, whisking as you go. Carry on whisking as you shower in the sugar.

Place the bowl over the saucepan, making sure that the bottom of the bowl is not in direct contact with the water. Continue whisking the mixture over the heat so that it gradually thickens, making sure that the temperature of the water in the pan increases steadily but moderately.

Once it reaches the required temperature, the sabayon should have a very thick ribbon consistency and a fluffy, rich and shiny texture. Remove the bowl from the pan.

After 8–10 minutes, the mixture should have reached a light ribbon consistency. It is essential to keep whisking all the time. When the temperature reaches 55°C, the sabayon is cooked.

Serve the sabayon immediately, in glasses. Or spoon it over a medley of red fruits or fruit-filled crêpes in a gratin dish and place under a hot grill until the sabayon is lightly browned.

kirsch sabayon with seasonal fruits

A heavenly marriage of sweetness, freshness and elegance, with the sabayon gently caressing the fruit…

sabayon
75ml kirsch
3 egg yolks
80g caster sugar

fruit
2 oranges, segmented
1 pear, peeled, cored, sliced and sprinkled
with lemon juice
20 blackberries

One-third fill a saucepan (large enough to hold the base of a heatproof, large round-bottomed bowl) with warm water. Put the kirsch, 50ml water, the egg yolks and sugar in the bowl and place over the saucepan, making sure the bowl isn't touching the water. Whisk with a balloon whisk.

Place the saucepan over a low heat and whisk the mixture constantly for 8–10 minutes, until the sabayon is a creamy ribbon consistency, making sure that the temperature increases slowly but steadily. Continue whisking until the mixture reaches 55°C, then take the bowl off the heat. The sabayon will now be a very thick ribbon consistency, with a foamy, rich and shiny texture; it is now ready to serve.

Divide the fruit between 4 glass dishes and coat with the sabayon. Serve at once, with the rest of the sabayon in a pouring jug.

grapefruit and ginger sabayon
Peel and grate 100g very fresh root ginger, then wrap it in muslin. Prepare the sabayon as above, replacing the kirsch with 50ml freshly squeezed grapefruit juice and squeezing as much juice from the ginger as possible into the mixture before whisking. Serve with rambutan or lightly grilled pineapple.

coffee crème caramel

serves 6

Fresh, sweet and bitter overtones all join forces in this sublime dessert, where coffee provides both the dominant flavour and the *bellissimo* finishing touch.

caramel
120g caster sugar
30g liquid glucose (optional)

crème
250ml milk
20g coffee beans, finely ground
100ml whipping cream
3 eggs, plus 3 egg yolks
60g caster sugar
10g coffee beans, crushed, to serve

For the caramel, dissolve the sugar in 2 tbsp water in a small, heavy-based pan and bring gently to the boil. Use a brush dipped in cold water to brush down any crystals forming on the side of the pan. Add the glucose, if using. Cook gently to a light caramel. Divide between 6 ceramic or metal moulds, about 7cm in diameter and 3.5cm high, rotating each, so the caramel coats two-thirds of the way up the sides. Stand in a shallow roasting dish lined with greaseproof paper. Preheat the oven to 120°C/Gas ½.

For the crème, bring the milk and ground coffee to the boil in a pan, then add the cream and return to the boil. Take off the heat and set aside to infuse. Gently whisk the eggs, egg yolks and sugar together in a bowl for 1 minute. Slowly strain the boiling hot coffee milk through a fine sieve onto the egg and sugar mix, stirring with a balloon whisk as you do so. Use a skimmer to remove any bubbles from the surface.

Fill the caramel-lined moulds with the mixture, to about 5mm from the rim. Pour enough hot water into the roasting dish to come halfway up the sides of the moulds. Place carefully in the oven and cook for 50 minutes or until lightly set. Transfer the moulds to a wire rack to cool, then chill for 4 hours.

To turn out, dip the base of each mould in boiling water for 10 seconds, then invert over a shallow bowl. Spoon any caramel left in the moulds over each crème caramel. Sprinkle the crushed coffee beans around the base. Serve cold but not overly chilled.

crema catalana

serves 4–6

750ml milk, ideally goat's, but cow's is fine
1 generous tsp crushed fennel seeds
1 small cinnamon stick, broken into pieces
150g caster sugar
very finely grated zest of 1 lemon
very finely grated zest of 1 orange
2 whole eggs, plus 6 egg yolks
40g cornflour
80g demerara or soft brown sugar

Put the milk, fennel seeds, cinnamon and 100g of the caster sugar in a saucepan and bring to the boil. As soon as it boils, add the citrus zests. Take off the heat, cover and leave to infuse for 5–10 minutes.

Put the eggs, egg yolks and remaining 50g caster sugar into a bowl and mix with a balloon whisk for 30 seconds. Add the cornflour and mix well.

Slowly strain the milk through a chinois or sieve into the egg mixture, stirring with a whisk as you do so, then return to the pan.

This dessert, from Catalonia in Spain, is one of my favourites. You can make the cremas a day ahead and keep them in the fridge. Caramelise just before serving.

Cook the mixture over a gentle heat for 3 minutes, until thickened, stirring all the time with a whisk.

Sprinkle half the demerara or brown sugar evenly over the cremas, then wave a cook's blowtorch over the surface to caramelise lightly, or place briefly under a hot grill. Wait 5 minutes, then repeat to create a generous caramel layer.

Spoon into shallow individual dishes, about 14cm in diameter and 3cm deep, smoothing it lightly and evenly with the back of the spoon. Leave to cool, then chill in the fridge for at least 2 hours.

Serve at once, to fully appreciate the contrast of the warm, crisp caramel and the cold crema underneath.

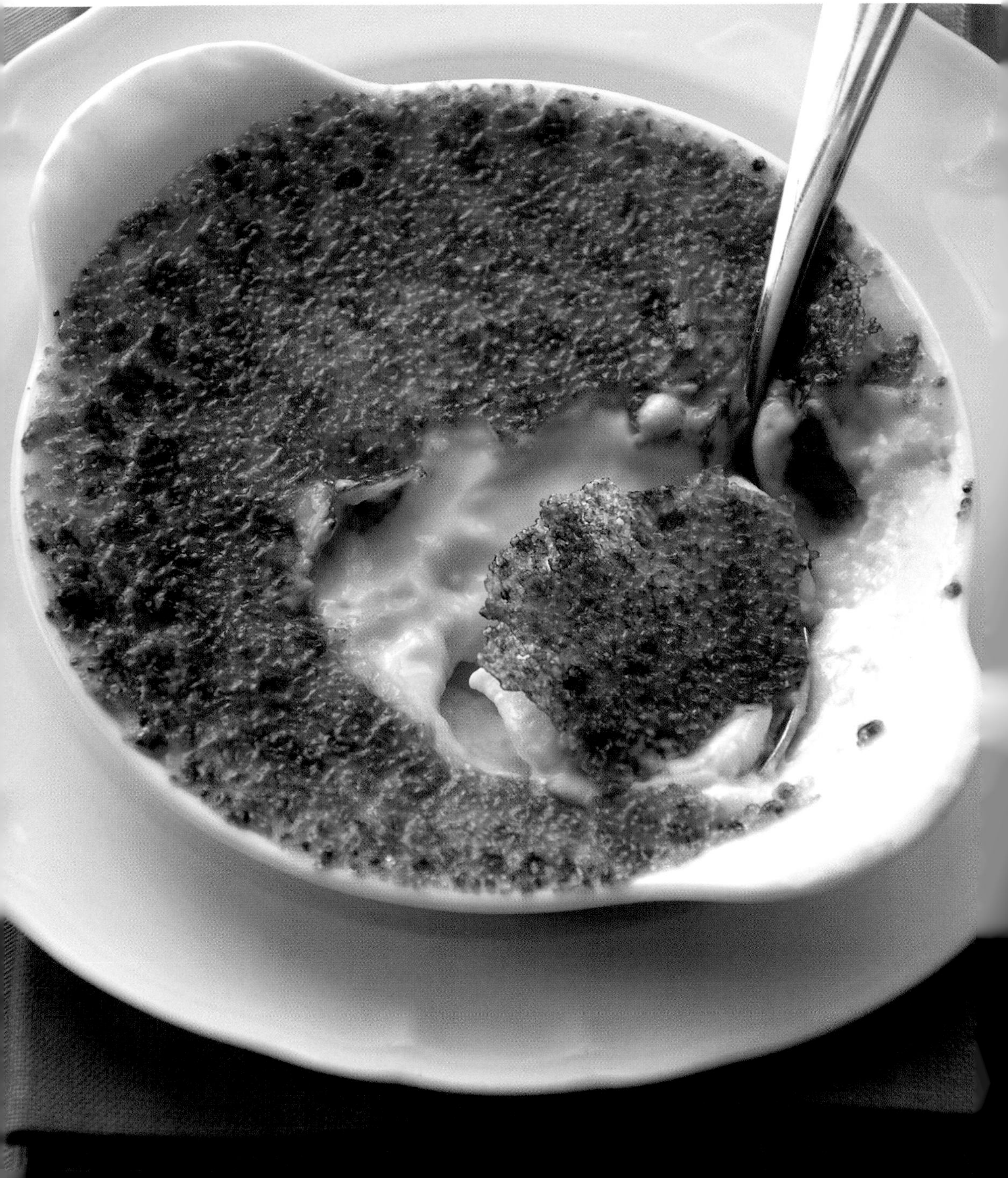

serves 6–8

In its classic form, crème brûlée is on the rich side, but this version is
fresh-tasting and easy to digest, thanks to the ginger.

80g very fresh root ginger
500ml milk
500ml whipping cream
150g caster sugar
200g egg yolks (about 10 eggs)
70g demerara sugar
80g preserved stem ginger in syrup, finely diced
   (optional)

Preheat the oven to 100°C/Gas ½. Peel the root ginger, grate it finely, then place
in a square of muslin and squeeze out as much juice as possible into a small dish.

Put the milk, cream and 90g of the caster sugar into a pan and heat, stirring
regularly with a balloon whisk, until the sugar is dissolved, then bring slowly to the
boil. Meanwhile, lightly whisk the egg yolks and remaining caster sugar in a bowl.

As soon as the milk and cream mixture comes to the boil, pour it a little at a time
onto the egg yolks and sugar, whisking all the time, then add the ginger juice.

Divide the mixture between individual gratin dishes about 15cm in diameter. Cook
in the oven for 50–55 minutes, or until very lightly set and still wobbly in the middle.
Place the dishes on a wire rack and leave to cool, then refrigerate until ready to serve.

Just before serving, sprinkle the demerara sugar over the surface of the crème brûlées
and caramelise, either using a cook's blowtorch or under a very hot grill, until a fine,
pale, nut-brown crust has formed. Top with the preserved ginger dice, if using, and
serve at once.

fig and honey pannacotta

serves 6–8

Honey adds a lovely dimension, but if you are concerned about upsetting the purity of the flavour, use sugar instead. If you wish to turn out the pannacottas to serve, oil the moulds and use an extra ½ leaf of gelatine – they will look pretty, but the texture won't be quite as delicate.

1½ sheets leaf gelatine
300ml double cream
200ml milk
100g runny honey, or 80g caster sugar
2 vanilla pods, split lengthways
3 ripe fresh figs, sliced into fine rounds

Soak the gelatine in cold water to cover for about 5 minutes. Heat the cream, milk, honey or sugar and vanilla pods in a saucepan, stirring from time to time, until the mixture almost reaches the boil, then remove from the heat. Immediately drain the gelatine and squeeze out excess water, then add to the creamy milk, stirring until completely melted.

Strain the mixture through a fine sieve or chinois into a bowl. Stand in a larger bowl filled with ice cubes and a little water to cool quickly, stirring from time to time, until it is nearly cold.

Meanwhile, arrange fig slices around the sides of 6–8 individual glass bowls or cups (measuring about 8cm across the top), making sure they adhere; save 6–8 slices for decoration. Carefully pour in the pannacotta mixture, ensuring it covers the figs. Refrigerate until set, at least 2 hours, or overnight if preparing ahead.

Remove from the fridge about 10 minutes before serving. Top each pannacotta with a fig slice to serve.

espresso vanilla pannacotta
Omit the figs. At the table, pour a strong, piping hot espresso over each pannacotta… a real explosion of flavours.

tiramisu verrine with marrons glacés

serves 6

This delectable dessert from Italy is universally popular. When strawberries are at the peak of their season and bursting with sweetness and flavour, I substitute them for the marrons glacés.

3 egg yolks
90g caster sugar
200g mascarpone
200ml whipping cream
60g icing sugar
3 very strong espresso measure coffees, cooled

1 tbsp sambuca (or other anise liqueur)
6 sponge fingers (page 279), or use
   shop-bought
6 marrons glacés, cut in half
   horizontally
40g good-quality cocoa powder

Whisk the egg yolks and sugar together in a bowl until smooth, pale and thickened to a ribbon consistency. Whisk in the mascarpone.

In a separate bowl, whip the cream with the icing sugar to firm peaks. Fold into the mascarpone mixture, using a rubber spatula, taking care to avoid overworking. As soon as the mixture is evenly combined, cover and set aside in the fridge.

Pour the cold espresso coffee and sambuca into a shallow dish (wide enough to take the sponge fingers).

To assemble the tiramisus, spoon one-third of the creamy mascarpone mixture into 6 serving glasses, dividing it equally. Pick out the 6 least perfect marron glacé halves and crumble them into the glasses.

Now, dip the sponge fingers into the coffee mixture, 2 or 3 at a time, for a few seconds, turning them to allow both sides to absorb the liquid, then lift out and arrange on top of the desserts. Press the biscuits very lightly with your fingertips. Divide the remaining creamy mixture between the glasses, tapping them lightly on the work surface to level. Refrigerate for at least 3 hours before serving.

To serve, dust the surface of each tiramisu generously with cocoa powder and gently place a marron glacé half on top of each.

This dessert really couldn't be simpler to make, and its velvety texture
and fresh burst of lemon never fail to delight and surprise.

6 lemons
375g caster sugar
700ml double cream
30g skinned pistachio nuts, coarsely chopped

Wash 2 lemons in cold water, wipe dry, then use a fine zester to remove the zest. Put
the zest strips on a plate in the microwave on full power to dry for 10 seconds, then
set aside in a dry place.

Cut all 6 lemons in half and squeeze out the juice. Strain the juice through a fine
sieve into a saucepan, add the sugar and place over a gentle heat, stirring constantly
with a wooden spoon until the sugar has completely dissolved. Remove from the
heat and set aside.

Bring the cream to the boil in a heavy-based pan, then immediately pour in the
lemon syrup, stirring with a wooden spoon. Strain the mixture through a fine sieve
or chinois into a jug.

Divide the posset between 6 glasses or glass serving dishes and refrigerate for at
least 4 hours.

To serve, sprinkle the reserved lemon zest and chopped pistachios over the surface
of each dessert and serve immediately.

Here are two worlds to visit: one of light, billowy soufflés that emanate an air of mystery… for the uninitiated. They are in fact easy to master, particularly if you follow the step-by-step photographs on the following pages. I want to encourage you to be bold and jump right in – you'll be surprised at what you can do. The other world is one of comforting puddings, which may seem a little old-fashioned, especially to those who haven't experienced the best of them. For me, they are some of the desserts that I most love to make for my family and friends, more often than not at their request.

hot soufflés
&puddings

orange soufflés

serves 4

These beautiful individual soufflés taste as good as they look and they are not difficult to make.

40g butter, softened, to grease
70g caster sugar, plus an extra 40g to coat
  the dishes
250ml freshly squeezed orange juice
125ml milk
3 egg yolks, plus 6 egg whites
10g plain flour
10g cornflour
very finely grated zest of 2 oranges
30ml Grand Marnier (optional)
20–30g icing sugar, to dust

Brush 4 ramekins or small soufflé dishes, about 8cm in diameter and 6cm high, with the butter. Put the 40g caster sugar in one of the buttered dishes and rotate it at an angle so that the sugar coats the inside entirely, then tip the excess into the next dish, tapping it as you do so. Repeat until all the dishes are coated. Simmer the orange juice in a pan over a medium heat, to reduce by half to 125ml.

Slowly bring the milk to the boil in a saucepan over a gentle heat, then whisk in the reduced orange juice and continue whisking until it returns to the boil.

Whisk the egg yolks and 20g of the caster sugar together in a bowl for 1 minute, then add the flour and cornflour and whisk for a further minute. Pour on the boiling milk and orange juice, whisking all the time, then mix in the orange zest.

The Grand Marnier accentuates the fragrant orange flavours, but it's up to you whether you include it or not.

Preheat the oven to 190°C/Gas 5. In a clean bowl, whisk the egg whites to soft peaks. Gradually whisk in the remaining 50g caster sugar. Using a whisk, incorporate one-third of the whites into the soufflé mixture, without overworking.

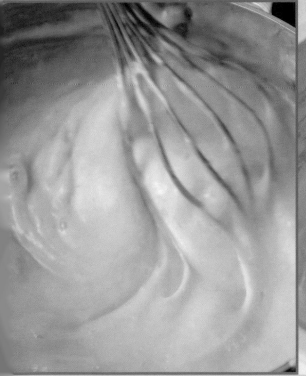

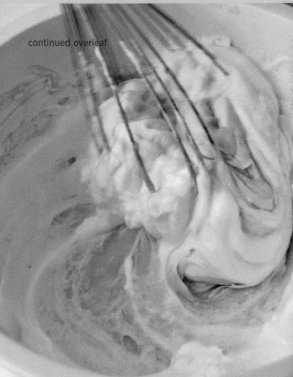

continued overleaf

Pour the mixture back into the pan and stir with a whisk over a gentle heat until it comes to the boil. Allow to boil gently for 1 minute, stirring, then add the Grand Marnier, if using. Pour the orange-flavoured crème patissière into a bowl, cover with cling film and set aside for 10 minutes.

Now gently fold in the remaining egg whites, using a rubber spatula, until the mixture is just smooth and homogeneous; take care not to overwork.

continued overleaf

Using a large spoon, divide the soufflé mixture between the prepared dishes, and give each a light tap on the work surface.

Slide the blade of a small knife around the inside edge of each dish, to give the soufflés a good shape as they rise in the oven. Bake for 7–8 minutes.

On removing from the oven, sprinkle the tops with icing sugar. Stand each dish on an individual plate lined with a napkin and serve at once.

Soufflés are simple to make and the technique is always the same. A base mixture, usually a crème patissière, is flavoured with a fruit purée, chocolate, alcohol etc., and lightened by folding in whisked egg whites. The mixture is baked in a straight-sided dish so it rises impressively.

Rhubarb soufflé Prepare 4 individual soufflé dishes, about 10cm in diameter and 6cm high (as for orange soufflés). Cut 200g young, tender rhubarb stalks into pieces, steam in a covered pan over a low heat until tender, then purée in a food processor or blender. Stir into 250g warm crème patissière (page 273). Whisk 8 egg whites with 20g caster sugar until semi-firm, then fold into the soufflé base. Use to fill the prepared dishes and bake as for orange soufflés. Serves 4

Chocolate and drambuie soufflé Prepare 4 individual soufflé dishes, about 10cm in diameter and 6cm high (as for orange soufflés). Stir 50ml Drambuie into 350g warm crème patissière (page 273). Whisk 8 egg whites with 20g caster sugar until semi-firm, then fold into the soufflé base. Shower in 80g finely chopped dark, bitter chocolate (ideally couverture) and fold in very lightly, just turning the spatula once or twice; do not overmix. Immediately fill the prepared dishes and bake as for orange soufflés. Serves 4

passion fruit and kiwi soufflé

serves 10

70g butter, softened, to grease
70g caster sugar, plus an extra 70g to coat
   the dishes
5–6 kiwi fruit
8–10 passion fruit
6 egg whites

crème patissière
4 egg yolks
50g caster sugar
25g plain flour
250ml milk

to finish
2 kiwi fruit, peeled and finely sliced
3 passion fruit, pulp and seeds scooped out

Brush the insides of 10 individual soufflé dishes, 10cm in diameter and 6cm high, with the softened butter. (Or use 16 smaller moulds, 8cm in diameter and 4cm high.) Add the 70g caster sugar to one of the buttered moulds and rotate it so that the sugar coats the entire inside of the mould. Tip the excess sugar into another mould and repeat. Continue until all the moulds are coated in sugar.

Peel the kiwi fruit, cut into chunks and then process in a food processor or blender for 30 seconds (no longer or the seeds will be crushed, producing a bitter juice). Pour into a fine sieve set over a bowl and press with a ladle to extract the juice. You will need about 45ml.

Halve the passion fruit, scoop the pulp and seeds out into the (clean) food processor or blender and blitz for 45 seconds. Pour into a fine sieve set over a bowl and press down with a ladle to extract the juice. You will need about 90ml.

For the crème patissière, whisk the egg yolks with one-third of the sugar in a bowl, until it reaches a ribbon consistency. Add the flour and mix in well. Heat the milk with the remaining two-thirds of the sugar in a large pan. As soon as it comes to the boil, add the passion fruit juice and heat again, whisking from time to time until it reaches the boil again. Immediately pour onto the egg yolk mixture, whisking all

illustrated on previous page

At the Waterside Inn, we often make these soufflés for 80 people at once… So be bold and give your guests a real treat. They are really not difficult to make but everyone will be amazed by your skill and expertise.

the time. Pour the mixture back into the pan and cook over a medium heat, stirring with a whisk, for 2 minutes. Pour into a bowl and set aside for 5 minutes to cool slightly. Pour the kiwi juice into the crème patissière, mixing well with a whisk.

Preheat the oven to 190°C/Gas 5. Whisk the egg whites in a clean bowl to soft peaks. Gradually whisk in the 70g sugar and continue to whisk until almost firm, but not overly stiff, peaks. Whisk one-third of the egg whites into the tepid crème patissière (at 40–50°C), then gently fold in the remaining two-thirds, using a rubber spatula.

Place the prepared dishes on a baking sheet lined with greaseproof paper and fill each with the soufflé mixture, using a large spoon. Smooth the tops with a palette knife, if necessary. Run the blade of a small knife around the inside of each dish, to detach the soufflé mixture from it, just a little. Bake in the oven for 7 minutes (or 5–6 minutes if using small dishes).

As soon as the soufflés are out of the oven, place a slice of kiwi on top of each and spoon some passion fruit pulp and seeds around the kiwi. Place each soufflé dish on a small plate lined with a small napkin and serve immediately.

NOTE The crème patissière can be made in advance and reheated in the microwave.

pear soufflés with pistachios

serves 8

These little soufflés are light and elegant, with a delicate pear aroma. I adore
the contrast of the crunchy pistachios and smooth, fluffy soufflé.

poached pears
200g caster sugar
juice of 1 lemon
4 perfectly ripe pears

soufflé mix
30g potato flour
150ml Poire William (pear) eau-de-vie
50g butter, softened, to grease
25g caster sugar, plus 50g to coat the dishes
4 medium egg whites

to decorate
32 pistachio nuts, skinned and coarsely chopped

To poach the pears, pour 500ml water into a medium pan, add the sugar and lemon
juice, dissolve over a medium heat and bring to the boil. Peel, halve and core the pears.
Add to the pan and simmer for about 10 minutes, until lightly soft. Tip the pears and
all but 200ml syrup into a bowl. Over a high heat, reduce the syrup in the pan by half.

Put 6 pear halves in a blender with the reduced syrup and process to a purée; keep
the other 2 pear halves in the remaining syrup. Tip the purée into a small pan. Mix
the potato flour with the eau-de-vie, stir into the purée and cook over a low heat for
4–5 minutes, stirring constantly. Turn into a bowl, cover with cling film and set aside.

Preheat the oven to 180°C/Gas 4. Brush the insides of 8 dariole moulds, about 8cm
high and 5cm across the top, with the butter. Tip 50g sugar into a mould and rotate
it to coat the inside. Tip the excess into the next mould. Repeat to coat all of them.

Whisk the egg whites in a bowl to soft peaks. Add the 25g sugar and whisk until
almost firm. Whisk one-third into the pear mixture to loosen it, then use a spatula to
gently fold in the rest. Fill the dariole moulds almost to the brim with the soufflé mix
and bake in the oven for 4 minutes. Meanwhile, dice the remaining 2 pear halves.

Protecting your hand with a cloth, turn the soufflés out onto plates. Surround with the
diced pear, spooning over a little of the syrup. Sprinkle with the pistachios and serve.

warm chocolate fondants

serves 10–12

200g butter, softened, plus 20g to grease
200g good-quality dark, bitter or Manjari chocolate,
    preferably Valrhona, finely chopped
200g icing sugar, sifted, plus extra to dust
4 eggs, mixed with an extra 4 egg yolks
55g plain flour
35g dark, bitter cocoa powder
500ml warm coffee crème anglaise (page 58),
    to serve

Use a brush to lightly butter the insides of 12 metal rings, 5cm in diameter and 3.5cm high and line each with a band of greaseproof paper, 5cm high (shown on page 94). Stand the rings on a baking tray lined with greaseproof paper.

Preheat the oven to 190°C/Gas 5. Put the chocolate into a heatproof bowl and set over a saucepan one-third filled with hot water, making sure the bottom of the bowl is not in contact with the water. Place over a gentle heat until the chocolate has melted, then take off the heat and set aside in a warm place.

Using an electric whisk, beat the butter and icing sugar together until pale and aerated, then slowly incorporate the eggs, whisking constantly to keep the mixture smooth. Reduce the mixer speed and incorporate the melted chocolate a little at a time. Sift the flour and cocoa together over the mixture and fold in carefully, using a large metal spoon.

Fill the prepared moulds with the fondant mixture to the top of the rings.

illustrated on previous page

Fondants vary enormously, but these are the best I've ever tasted. This is my adaptation of a recipe belonging to our skilful English pâtisserie mascot, Claire Clark, first female holder of the prestigious 'Meilleur Ouvrier de la Grande-Bretagne', a true artist and dear friend.

Bake in the oven for 8–10 minutes. To check to see if they are done, insert a small skewer into the centre of one; if the centre feels liquid, it is not yet cooked. If it feels soft, and the skewer meets with no resistance, they are done – the centre should still be very slightly runny. Remove from the oven and leave to rest on the baking tray for 30 seconds.

Lift the rings off all the fondants, slide a small palette knife under one, transfer it to a serving plate and remove the band of greaseproof paper. Repeat with the rest of the fondants. Dust the tops with icing sugar, pour coffee crème anglaise around each fondant and serve immediately.

NOTE Ramekins can be used in place of metal rings. Simply un-mould directly onto the plates.

If you have a portion of brioche dough, use it here, otherwise pain perdu – literally 'lost bread' – is an excellent way to use up a good panettone. Serve with a fresh apple coulis (page 23), to cut through the wicked richness.

600g brioche dough (page 278) plus
    120g sultanas, or 500g shop-bought
    panettone
1 egg yolk, mixed with 2 tsp milk, to glaze
250ml cold milk
50ml crème fraîche

30g caster sugar
1 whole egg, plus 1 egg yolk
pinch of salt
140g butter
50g granulated sugar to sprinkle, or 50ml maple
    syrup to drizzle, plus extra to serve

If using brioche dough, knead in the sultanas, then shape into a roll, 3cm in diameter, on a lightly floured surface and place on a baking tray. (Or make a longer roll, 1.5cm in diameter and form a plait.) Leave for 1½ hours, at about 24°C, (an airing cupboard is ideal) until nearly doubled in size. Preheat the oven to 200°C/Gas 6.

Brush the brioche with the glaze. If it's not plaited, snip the top at 2cm intervals, to a 1cm depth with kitchen scissors dipped in cold water. Bake for 10 minutes, then lower the setting to 170°C/Gas 3 and bake for a further 20 minutes. Cool on a wire rack.

Put the milk, crème fraîche, sugar, egg, egg yolk and salt into a bowl and mix together lightly, using a balloon whisk. Cut the brioche or panettone into at least 8 slices, about 1.5cm thick. Pour the milk and egg mix into a shallow dish large enough to fit all the brioche slices. Lay the slices in the dish to soak and turn them over after 2 minutes.

In a large frying pan, preferably non-stick, heat 80g of the butter. When it begins to foam, lay the brioche slices in the pan. After 1 minute, add the remaining butter in little pieces in between the brioche slices, and turn the slices over; they should be light brown in colour. Cook for 1–2 minutes on the other side until nicely golden, then sprinkle with the granulated sugar or drizzle over the maple syrup.

Place 2 slices on each plate and serve at once, with extra sugar or maple syrup.

These individual rice puddings are soft, gooey in the middle and delicate, with the mandarin contributing a refreshing hint of citrus.

750ml milk
75g short-grain pudding rice
8 cardamom pods, crushed and tied
   in muslin
6 egg yolks
75g caster sugar

caramel
120g caster sugar
30g liquid glucose (optional)

to serve
8 mandarins

Bring the milk to the boil in a pan, then tip in the rice. Add the cardamom. Cook over a gentle heat for 15 minutes, stirring from time to time. Take off the heat, cover and set aside for 10 minutes. Whisk the egg yolks and sugar together in a large bowl. Discard the cardamom from the rice and milk, then stir into the whisked mixture.

For the caramel, dissolve the sugar in 2 tbsp water in a small, heavy-based pan and bring gently to the boil. Use a brush dipped in cold water to brush down any crystals that form on the side of the pan. Add the glucose, if using. Cook gently to a light caramel. Divide between 8 ceramic or metal moulds, 7cm in diameter and 3.5cm high, rotating each, so the caramel coats two-thirds of the way up the sides. Stand in a shallow roasting dish lined with greaseproof paper. Preheat the oven to 120°C/Gas ½.

Divide the rice mix between the moulds. Pour enough hot water into the roasting dish to come halfway up the sides of the moulds. Transfer carefully to the oven and cook for 50 minutes, until set. Transfer the moulds to a wire rack to cool, then chill for 4 hours.

Over a bowl to catch the juice, peel and segment the mandarins, removing all pith and membrane. Squeeze the membranes to extract as much juice as possible. To turn out the puddings, dip the base of each mould in boiling water for 10 seconds, then invert onto a plate. Add any caramel left in the moulds to the mandarin juice, stir, then spoon around the puddings. Arrange the mandarin segments in the juice.

steamed sussex pond pudding

serves 6–8

illustrated on previous page

I adore this comforting winter pudding. It may not be sophisticated in terms of presentation, but it is truly delicious. I like to serve it with a jug of warm crème anglaise (page 56) or whipping cream.

suet dough
500g plain flour
15g baking powder
250g shredded suet (such as Atora)
140ml milk
pinch of fine salt

filling
250g butter, cut into dice, plus extra
  (softened) to grease
250g demerara sugar
1 large, thin-skinned lemon

Mix the flour, baking powder and suet together in a large bowl, using your fingertips. Add 140ml water, the milk and salt, and work the mixture with your hands until it forms a soft, even dough. Cover the bowl with a tea towel and refrigerate for 30 minutes.

Lightly butter a 1 litre pudding basin. On a lightly floured surface, gently roll out three-quarters of the dough to a circle, 1cm thick, and use to line the prepared pudding basin, pressing it gently against the sides.

Using fingertips, roughly mix the butter with the sugar and tip into the lined basin. Prick the lemon a dozen times with a fork, and push it into the butter-sugar mix.

Roll out the other piece of dough to a circle about 18cm in diameter. Brush the top edge of the dough lining the basin with water, then position the dough circle on top, to form a lid. Using your thumb and index finger, pinch the edges together to seal.

Cover the basin with a circle of greaseproof paper, pleated in the centre to allow room for expansion, and then with a round of pleated foil. Secure under the rim with kitchen string. Place in a large saucepan and pour in enough boiling water to come halfway up the side of the basin. Cover tightly and steam for 3 hours, topping up with boiling water as necessary; don't let it boil dry.

Uncover the pudding, turn out onto a large serving plate and serve immediately.

serves 4–6

This classic English family pudding separates delectably into
a sponge layer on top and a creamy, lemony sauce underneath.
My brother, Albert, used to make it often in the 1960s.

45g butter, softened, plus 20g to grease
240g caster sugar
finely grated zest of 1 lemon
2 eggs, separated
3 tbsp self-raising flour
300ml milk
juice of 1½ lemons

Butter a 16cm round ovenproof dish (or an oval dish of similar capacity.)

Put the butter, 220g of the sugar and the lemon zest in a bowl and beat, using a whisk,
for 1 minute. Add the egg yolks and beat until the mixture is very smooth. Incorporate
the flour and milk a little at time, alternating them, until the mixture is smooth and
homogeneous. Whisk in the lemon juice.

In another bowl, whisk the egg whites to soft peaks. Add the remaining 20g sugar and
whisk to fairly firm peaks. Using a rubber spatula, gently fold the egg whites into the
pudding mixture, without overworking it. Pour the mixture into the prepared dish.

Stand the dish in a shallow roasting tray, lined with greaseproof paper, then pour
enough hot water (at about 60°C) into the tray to come halfway up the side of the dish.
Carefully transfer to the oven and cook for 55 minutes, until well risen and golden.

Leave the pudding to stand for 10 minutes before serving.

I like to accompany this pudding with a redcurrant coulis (page 20), or with
a jug of thick pouring cream.

These evoke such childhood memories — treasured moments in the folds of my mother's apron as she lovingly prepared them – then the magical time around the table, savouring them piping hot. These desserts from my mother's – even grandmother's – era are enjoyed as much today as ever. I find them irresistible and never tire of them. Inexpensive and quick to prepare, their simple aromas will fill the room and stimulate the taste buds in a pleasingly singular way.

crêpes, batters & beignets

crêpes

makes 16–18

125g plain flour
15g caster sugar
pinch of salt
2 eggs
325ml milk
100ml double cream
few drops of vanilla extract or orange flower
    water, or a little grated lemon zest
20g clarified butter (page 283), to cook

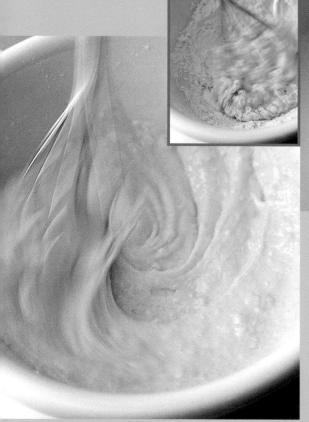

To make the batter, put the flour, sugar and salt into a bowl. Add the eggs, mix well with a whisk, then stir in 100ml milk to make a smooth batter. Gradually stir in the rest of the milk and the cream. Leave the batter to rest in a warm place for about an hour.

When you are ready to cook the crêpes, give the batter a stir and flavour with vanilla, orange flower water or lemon zest. Brush a 22cm crêpe pan with a little clarified butter and heat. Ladle in a little batter and tilt the pan to cover the base thinly. Cook the crêpe for about 1 minute.

As soon as little holes appear on the surface, turn the crêpe over and cook the other side for 30–40 seconds. Transfer to a plate and cook the rest of the batter, stacking the crêpes interleaved with greaseproof paper as they are cooked.

Dust the crêpes with sugar, sprinkle liberally with lemon juice, then roll up or fold into quarters and eat straight away. Or fill as suggested overleaf.

crêpes with almond cream Preheat the oven to 180°C/Gas 4. Whisk 180g crème patissière (page 273) with 300g frangipane (page 273) until smooth, then flavour with 50ml dark rum if you like. Lay 8 crêpes on your work surface and spread with the almond filling, leaving a 1.5cm margin around the edge. Fold each crêpe in half, then in half again, to give a quarter circle. Lay the filled crêpes on a lightly buttered baking tray, sprinkle liberally with 30g icing sugar and place in the oven for 5 minutes to melt and lightly caramelise the icing sugar; if necessary, place for a few seconds under a hot grill. Serve immediately. Serves 8

crêpes with summer berries Have ready a quantity of raspberry or blackberry coulis (page 21). Lay a warm crêpe on each of 8 warm plates. Scatter over 150g each raspberries and blackberries. Cover each serving with another crêpe and fold it back slightly to reveal the fruit. Spoon on the red berry coulis and serve immediately, dusted with icing sugar. Serves 8

banana soufflé crêpes with chocolate sauce

serves 8

4 perfectly ripe, medium bananas
juice of ½ lemon
50ml milk
3 egg yolks
60g caster sugar
1 tbsp potato flour

7 egg whites
8 crêpes (page 108), trimmed
  to about 16cm diameter
30g butter, to grease
½ quantity chocolate sauce
  (page 274)

Preheat the oven to 190°C/Gas 5. Put the bananas, unpeeled, on a baking tray and cook in the oven for 5 minutes. Turn them over and cook for a further 5 minutes; the skin will be black when you remove them from the oven. Set aside to cool for 10 minutes.

Using a small knife, remove the skins from the bananas and press the flesh through a sieve or fine mouli, to give you 350–400g purée. Put the banana purée into a small saucepan with the lemon juice, stir with a whisk and add the milk. Bring to the boil over a gentle heat, stirring every minute or so.

Meanwhile, whisk the egg yolks with 20g of the caster sugar in a small bowl. After 1 minute, add the potato flour and mix well, then pour this into the boiling banana and milk mixture, stirring with a balloon whisk. Simmer, still stirring, for 1 minute. Remove from the heat, cover with cling film and set aside. Lower the oven setting to 180°C/Gas 4.

illustrated on previous page

This recipe is tricky to make successfully in smaller quantities. If there are four of you, my advice is simply to eat two crêpes each. You will easily manage to do so – they are light, taste divine and are deliciously indulgent.

In a clean bowl, whisk the egg whites to soft peaks. Add the remaining 40g caster sugar and continue to whisk to firm peaks, making sure they are not overly stiff. Using a balloon whisk, incorporate one-third of the whisked egg whites into the cooled banana mixture, then gently fold in the remainder, using a rubber spatula.

Place each crêpe on a small piece of lightly buttered baking parchment on a baking sheet. Drop a generous spoonful of banana soufflé mixture on one half of each crêpe, then use a palette knife to fold the other half of the crêpe over the soufflé to enclose it, without pressing down (shown on page 112). Place in the oven for 5 minutes.

As soon as the crêpes come out of the oven, use a large palette knife to transfer them carefully, one at a time, from the greaseproof paper to warmed serving plates. Drizzle a little chocolate sauce decoratively over each crêpe and serve immediately. Offer the remaining chocolate sauce on the side.

parcels of poached pears

serves 6

Crisp on the outside, meltingly soft within, these hot little parcels are delectable. They can be prepared several hours in advance, up to the stage where you cook them, and the pears can be poached a day ahead.

500g caster sugar
8 cloves
4 perfectly ripe pears
300g rough puff pastry (page 281)
6 crêpes, 18–20cm in diameter (page 108)
8 fresh mint leaves, finely snipped
grapeseed or groundnut oil, to deep-fry
granulated sugar, to dust

Put 500ml water into a saucepan with the sugar and cloves and bring to the boil over a gentle heat. Keep the syrup at a bare simmer (90°C). Peel, halve and core the pears, then add to the syrup and poach gently for 10 minutes. Remove from the heat and leave the pears to cool in the syrup. Once cooled, place in the fridge.

On a lightly floured surface, roll out half the pastry as thinly as possible, no more than 2mm thick. Transfer to a baking sheet lined with greaseproof paper and refrigerate. Roll out the remaining pastry in the same way, then layer on the other rolled-out sheet in the fridge, with a sheet of greaseproof paper in between.

Drain the pears and cut into 2cm dice. Cut the crêpes into pieces just big enough to wrap the pear pieces. Roll each pear dice in snipped mint, then wrap in a crêpe piece. Cut the pastry into 8cm squares. Place a crêpe-covered piece of pear in the centre of each pastry square, then bring the sides of the square up over the top and pinch the edges together to seal. Refrigerate for 10 minutes.

Heat the oil in a deep-fat fryer or deep, heavy saucepan to 170°C. Cook the parcels, in batches of 8–10 at a time, in the hot oil for 4–5 minutes, until nutty brown in colour and crisp. Drain on kitchen paper; keep hot while cooking the rest.

Serve the little parcels hot, dusted with granulated sugar.

red berry beignets

serves 6–8

Light, with just a hint of a crunch as you bite into them, these beignets are lovely with a jug of red berry coulis (pages 20–1) on the side.

batter
7g fresh yeast
75ml milk, plus a little extra if needed
130g plain flour
pinch of salt
60ml light beer
1 egg, separated
2 tbsp groundnut oil
20g caster sugar

to cook and serve
grapeseed oil, to deep-fry
500g mixed red fruits, such as large
    strawberries (hulls intact), large blackberries,
    cherries (with stalks)
granulated or caster sugar, to serve

To make the batter, in a small bowl, whisk the yeast into one-third of the milk. Put the flour and salt into a large bowl and slowly pour in the rest of the milk, the beer and egg yolk, mixing continuously with a balloon whisk. Once the mixture is smooth, add the yeast and milk mixture with the groundnut oil. Mix to combine, then cover the bowl with cling film and leave to stand for at least 2 hours.

When almost ready to serve, in a clean bowl, whisk the egg white with the 20g sugar to firm peaks. Fold this into the batter, without overworking.

Heat the grapeseed oil in a deep-fat fryer or deep, heavy pan to 160–170°C. To test the consistency of the batter, using a fork, dip a single fruit into it to coat then immerse in the hot oil and deep-fry for 1½–2 minutes. Using a slotted spoon, remove and drain on kitchen paper. Cut the beignet in half; if the coating appears to be too thick, add ½–1 tbsp milk to the batter.

Deep-fry 6–8 individual fruits at a time, dipping each first in the batter before adding to the oil and cooking for 1½–2 minutes, until golden. Remove to a tray lined with kitchen paper to drain; keep warm while you deep-fry the remaining beignets. As soon as they are all cooked, sprinkle the beignets with a little sugar and serve.

4 eggs
160g plain flour
160g butter, melted and cooled
300ml milk
120g caster sugar
2 vanilla pods, split lengthways
60g butter
400g perfectly ripe cherries, stoned
generous pinch of granulated sugar, to sprinkle

Preheat the oven to 200°C/Gas 6. Lightly beat the eggs in a bowl, with a fork, then lightly beat in the flour. Whisk in the cooled melted butter, then gradually whisk in the milk followed by the sugar. With the point of a knife, scrape out the seeds from the vanilla pods and add them to the mixture.

Cut 20g of the butter into small pieces; set aside. Use the remaining 40g to generously grease an ovenproof dish, about 22cm in diameter and 3–4cm deep. Spread the cherries evenly over the base of the dish, then pour the batter mixture over them.

Carefully transfer the dish to the oven and bake for 10 minutes, then lower the oven setting to 180°C/Gas 4 and cook for a further 15 minutes or so. Scatter the reserved butter pieces evenly over the top of the clafoutis and bake for another 5 minutes, or until set. To check, carefully insert the point of a sharp knife in the middle; if it comes out clean, the clafoutis is cooked.

Sprinkle with the granulated sugar and leave to stand for 5 minutes or so. Serve the clafoutis warm, from the baking dish.

You can use different fruits for this, according to the season. Plums are always delicious in a clafoutis, particularly greengages.

redcurrant crumpets

serves 10 (plus extra crumpets)

Crumpets freeze well so it's worth making twice as many
as you need – as I have here – and freezing the rest for another occasion.
Simply defrost and heat in the oven or toaster just before serving.

450g plain flour
14g fresh yeast
½ tsp bicarbonate of soda
10g salt
500ml stock syrup (page 275)
500g redcurrants, washed and drained
 (two-thirds de-stalked)
400g clotted or thick double cream
few white currant sprigs (optional), to serve

Put the flour into a large bowl and make a well in the middle. Dissolve the yeast in
500ml hand-hot water, then pour into the flour, mixing with a balloon whisk until
smooth. Cover the bowl with cling film and set aside in a warm place (ideally 20–22°C),
for an hour, until the mixture is spongy and aerated.

In a bowl, whisk together the bicarbonate of soda, salt and 60ml cold water, then
whisk into the crumpet batter, without overworking it. The crumpet batter needs
to be cooked as soon as possible after this stage – in 3 or 4 batches.

Heat a large non-stick frying pan. Butter 5 (or more) metal rings, 8cm diameter and
1.5cm high. Place them in the almost-hot pan and immediately pour in some batter,
to three-quarters fill each ring. Cook over a gentle heat for 7–8 minutes, then, using
a palette knife, turn the crumpets over, still in their rings, and cook for another
2 minutes. Transfer to a wire rack and remove the rings. Repeat to cook the rest.

Bring the stock syrup to the boil in a saucepan. Take off the heat, add the de-stalked
redcurrants and leave for 30 seconds. Drain carefully and tip into a bowl, returning the
syrup to the pan. Boil the syrup over a high heat to reduce by one-third, then allow to
cool to just warm. Pour half of it over the drained redcurrants.

Place a hot crumpet on each plate and spoon the poached fruit and a little of the reduced syrup on top. Add a generous spoonful of cream. Surround with the sprigs of redcurrants, and white currants, if you have some.

Serve the crumpets at once, while still hot, with the remaining syrup in a small jug on the side.

Of all desserts, these have the broadest appeal, as they are loved by everyone, from the very young to the very old. Using a base of milk, eggs, sugar and a little cream, ice creams are simply sublime. Sorbets and granitas are less rich and just as easy and quick to prepare. Like ice creams, they can be flavoured with fruit, sweet spices, fragrant herbs, liqueurs and other ingredients, to delight family and friends. Domestic ice-cream machines are more efficient and less cumbersome than they used to be so you really can't go wrong with these recipes.

ice creams, sorbets & granitas

vanilla ice cream serves 8

Adding double cream makes this classic ice cream extra rich and creamy, but you can make it without if you prefer.

1 quantity crème anglaise (page 56)
100ml double cream (optional)

When the crème anglaise is ready, pour it into a bowl and set over a larger bowl of ice to hasten the cooling, stirring from time to time to prevent a skin forming. When it is cold, remove the vanilla pod.

If you are using cream, stir it into the crème anglaise once it is cool.

Pour the mixture into an ice-cream maker and churn for about 20 minutes, until the ice cream is firm but still creamy.

Transfer the ice cream to a chilled freezerproof container and keep it in the freezer until ready to serve.

The texture of ice cream is best if it is served shortly after churning.

stem ginger ice cream Prepare the crème anglaise as for vanilla ice cream, omitting the vanilla. While still hot, pour it into a food processor, add 75g chopped preserved stem ginger (drained of syrup) and whiz for 1 minute. Strain through a chinois or sieve into a bowl and cool over ice, stirring occasionally. Stir in 30g desiccated coconut, then churn in the usual way. Serves 8

cinnamon ice cream Make as for vanilla ice cream, infusing the milk for the crème anglaise with a 20g cinnamon stick instead of the vanilla pod. Serves 8

lavender ice cream Prepare as for vanilla ice cream, infusing the milk for the crème anglaise with about 10 sprigs of fresh lavender (not in full blossom) instead of the vanilla pod. Serves 8

chocolate ice cream Put 150ml whole milk, 150ml double cream and 50g caster sugar in a saucepan and bring to the boil over a medium heat. Meanwhile, whisk 3 egg yolks with 30g caster sugar in a bowl. Pour on the hot milk mixture, whisking as you do so, then pour back into the pan. Cook over a low heat until lightly thickened. Immediately take off the heat and stir in 100g chopped dark chocolate (55–70% cocoa solids) and stir with a whisk until melted. Cool over ice, stirring occasionally, then churn in the usual way. Serves 6

frozen pineapple soufflé with blackberries

serves 8–10

illustrated on previous page

1 ripe pineapple, about 1kg
12 cloves
750ml stock syrup (page 275)
250g blackberries
½–1 tsp groundnut oil, to brush

1 sheet leaf gelatine
150g Italian meringue mixture (page 152)
150ml whipping cream
30ml kirsch
40g lightly toasted flaked almonds

Using a serrated knife, cut a 2cm slice from the base of the pineapple and a 3cm slice from the top, removing the leafy fronds. Cut off all the skin and prise out any little black 'eyes' that remain. Cut the peeled pineapple lengthways into 6 pieces and stud each one with 2 cloves.

Bring the stock syrup to the boil in a large saucepan, then add the pineapple. Lower the heat and poach at 80–90°C for 30 minutes. Take the pan off the heat and leave the pineapple pieces to cool in the syrup. Drain once cooled, reserving the syrup. Discard the cloves and cut away the pineapple core. From the most attractive pieces, cut 2 or 3 slices, 5mm thick, then cut these into smaller pieces; reserve for decoration.

Put the remaining pineapple into a blender or food processor and process for 2 minutes to a purée. Pass through a chinois or sieve into a bowl, pressing down with the back of a small ladle to extract as much purée as possible. Cover and refrigerate.

Put the blackberries and half of the reserved poaching syrup into a saucepan and bring to the boil over a medium heat. Lower the heat and poach at 80–90°C for 5 minutes. Remove from the heat and leave the berries to cool in the syrup. Once cold, put half of the berries with half of their poaching syrup into a blender or food processor and process for 1 minute, then strain through a fine sieve or chinois into a bowl. Cover and refrigerate this coulis, and the remaining blackberries in their syrup.

This impressive dessert is smooth, refreshing and utterly delicious. All the components can be prepared a day or two in advance, so on the day you just need to assemble it, which takes no time at all.

You will need a soufflé dish about 13cm in diameter and 8cm high. Fold a large piece of greaseproof paper in three lengthways (it needs to be long enough to go round the outside of the dish and wide enough to extend 6–8cm above the rim). Wrap the paper around the dish and secure it (as shown on page 130) with kitchen string. Lightly brush the inside of the paper above the rim with oil. Put the dish in the freezer.

Soak the gelatine in a dish of cold water for 5 minutes. Put the pineapple purée into a large bowl and whisk in the meringue. In another bowl, whip the cream to a ribbon consistency, then fold into the pineapple meringue mixture, using a rubber spatula.

Warm the kirsch slightly in a small pan, then take off the heat. Drain the gelatine, squeezing out excess water and add to the kirsch, stirring to dissolve. Fold into the soufflé mixture, without overworking. Take the dish from the freezer and fill with the mixture, to 4–5cm above the rim. Freeze for 3 hours, or refrigerate for 8 hours.

To serve, take off the string and carefully remove the paper collar. Scoop out 4 or 5 dessertspoonfuls from the middle of the soufflé, dipping the spoon in hot water before each scoop. Coat the reserved poached blackberries with two spoonfuls of the reserved blackberry coulis and use to fill the cavity. Arrange the reserved pineapple pieces around the top, alternating them with toasted flaked almonds. Serve at once, with the remaining blackberry coulis in a small jug on the side.

blood orange sorbet

170g caster sugar
30ml liquid glucose
1 dried red chilli, broken into pieces
1 thyme sprig
8 blood oranges

Put the sugar, liquid glucose and 200ml water in a pan over a medium heat. Bring to the boil, skim if necessary, then add the chilli and thyme. Boil for 30 seconds, then remove from the heat, cover and set aside to infuse. Once cold, strain through a fine sieve or chinois into a bowl and refrigerate.

Cut the oranges in half and squeeze out as much juice as possible. Strain through a sieve to remove any fibrous pulp and pips.

Pour the orange juice into the chilled syrup and stir briefly with a wooden spoon.

A sorbet should be on the tart side rather than overly sweet. You may need to adjust the quantity of sugar syrup according to how sweet or acidic the fruit is.

Start the ice-cream machine churning, then immediately pour in the sorbet mixture.

After 15–20 minutes, turn off the machine and use a spatula to bring the partially set sorbet around the sides into the middle. Churn for a further 10 minutes, or until the sorbet reaches a firm consistency. Turn the machine off.

Scoop the sorbet into serving glasses, using an ice-cream scoop dipped in cold water. Or, if not serving immediately, transfer to a suitable container and store in the freezer. For optimum flavour and texture, eat within a few days.

fruit sorbet variations

minted melon sorbet Blend 400g melon flesh with 8 fresh mint leaves, then strain through a fine sieve or chinois. Add 150ml stock syrup (page 275), the juice of 2 lemons and 2 turns of the black pepper mill (optional). Churn for 15–20 minutes. Serves 4

pineapple and cinnamon sorbet Purée 500g ripe pineapple flesh, then strain through a fine sieve or chinois into a bowl. Add 200ml stock syrup (page 275), the juice of 1 lemon and a good pinch of ground cinnamon. Churn for 15–20 minutes. Serve topped with slices of dried pineapple (page 16) for an impressive finish. Serves 4–6

A sorbet is best eaten freshly churned, when it will be meltingly smooth, but it can be stored in the freezer for up to a week, in a sealed container.

serves 6

When they are in season, raspberries or wild strawberries are
superb served with this delicately flavoured sorbet.

350ml stock syrup (page 275)
2 thyme sprigs
400g fromage frais (20–40% fat)
juice of 2 lemons, strained
¼ tsp finely ground white pepper, or to taste

Bring the stock syrup to the boil in a saucepan with the thyme sprigs added, then
take off the heat and leave to infuse for 2–3 minutes. Remove the thyme and set the
syrup aside to cool completely.

Put the fromage frais into a bowl and whisk in the cooled syrup, lemon juice and
pepper until evenly incorporated.

Start the ice-cream machine churning, then immediately pour in the sorbet mixture.
Churn for 15–20 minutes, until the sorbet reaches a firm consistency. Turn the
machine off. Unless serving straight away, transfer to a suitable container and
keep in the freezer.

The sorbet is best eaten within a few days. Scoop into glass dishes to serve.

chocolate sorbet

serves 6–8

100ml milk
150g caster sugar
40g liquid glucose
30g good-quality dark, bitter cocoa powder
100g dark chocolate couverture or good-quality
    dark chocolate, 70% cocoa solids (preferably
    Valrhona), chopped

to serve (optional)
6–8 meringue nests (page 149)

Put 400ml water into a saucepan with the milk, sugar, glucose and cocoa powder.
Bring to the boil over a medium heat, whisking with a balloon whisk. Lower the heat
and simmer for 2 minutes. Remove from the heat, add the chopped chocolate and stir
with a whisk for 2 minutes until melted. Strain through a fine sieve or chinois into a
bowl and set aside to cool, whisking from time to time. Cover and refrigerate.

Start the ice-cream machine churning, then immediately pour in the sorbet mixture.
Churn for 15–20 minutes, until thick. Turn the machine off. If not serving straight
away, transfer the sorbet to a suitable container and freeze.

When ready to serve, place a meringue nest, if serving, on each serving plate. Using
an ice-cream scoop dipped in hot water between each scoop so that the sorbet slides
out easily, scoop out a large ball for each meringue nest, placing it directly in the nest.
Alternatively, serve scoops of sorbet in individual glass bowls.

The contrast of dark with white, and of the crisp meringue with the soft
sorbet, makes this dessert particularly special. You can make the meringue
nests the day before, or if you prefer, serve the sorbet just as it is.

coffee and orange granitas in chocolate teardrops

serves 8

I love the bitter snap of chocolate with a granita and this elegant presentation will elicit a moment of stunned silence from your guests.

**400g good-quality dark chocolate, 70% cocoa
   solids (preferably Valrhona), chopped
300ml freshly made filter coffee (unsweetened)
5 oranges, washed
75g caster sugar**

Melt the chocolate in a heatproof bowl set over a pan of barely simmering water, making sure that the bottom of the bowl is not touching the water and stirring occasionally with a wooden spoon. The melted chocolate should be no hotter than 32°C. Remove the bowl from the pan.

To make the teardrops, cut 16 acetate strips, 26cm long and 4.5cm wide. Take a strip of acetate and slide it back and forth across the surface of the melted chocolate, to coat one side with chocolate from end to end. Place, uncoated side down, on a sheet of greaseproof paper. Repeat with the remaining acetate strips, then leave until beginning to set.

As the chocolate begins to set, take one of the strips and bend it, with the chocolate on the inside, to form a large teardrop shape. Secure the ends together with a small paper clip and set it down again on its side on the greaseproof paper (as shown on page 140). Repeat with the remaining chocolate-coated strips of acetate, to make 16 teardrops in total. Refrigerate for at least 30 minutes to set, or until ready to serve.

illustrated on previous page

You will need to cut strips from acetate sheets to shape the chocolate teardrops; these can be made a day ahead and kept in a cool place until ready to assemble.

For the coffee granita, pour the filter coffee into a shallow freezerproof container and freeze, stirring it with a fork every 30 minutes, until little flakes begin to form. This will take 2–3 hours.

For the orange granita, finely grate the zest from 1 orange. Halve and squeeze the juice from all 5 oranges. Tip the orange juice into a bowl, add the sugar and leave to dissolve (without heating) for about 10 minutes, stirring occasionally. Strain through a fine sieve or chinois into another bowl and add the grated zest. Pour into a shallow container and freeze, as for the coffee granita (above).

When ready to serve, one by one, remove the paper clip and carefully peel off the acetate strip from each chocolate teardrop, placing it straight onto a chilled serving plate and allowing two teardrops per serving. Using a strong spoon or fork, scrape shavings from the frozen coffee granita and use to fill one of the chocolate teardrops on each plate. In the same way, fill the other teardrop with orange granita shavings. Serve immediately.

This is a key chapter. French meringues are delicious just as they are, but the mixture also forms the basis for pavlova and other desserts. Italian meringue is an essential component in many classics, including mousses, charlottes and bavarois, where, in each case, the meringue brings a smooth lightness as well as shape and form to the dessert. Similarly, a Genoese sponge can be cooked and served in a variety of ways. On family summer holidays, I often bake a batch of sponges with my three granddaughters. The cakes are hardly out of the oven before we are tucking into them, with homemade jam.

sponges & meringues

french meringue

makes 275g, or 4–6 large meringues

Meringues are delicious served with
vanilla or chocolate ice cream.

3 egg whites
90g caster sugar
90g icing sugar, sifted

Add the icing sugar
and continue to beat
until the meringue
forms stiff peaks and
is smooth and shiny,
about 6–8 minutes.

Preheat the oven to 100°C/Gas ¼. Line a baking
sheet with baking parchment or a silicone liner.
Beat the egg whites in a clean bowl, using an
electric mixer, until softly peaking. Still whisking,
shower in the caster sugar and continue until the
mixture forms firm peaks.

Using a tablespoon, shape the meringues into 4–6 large quenelles and place on the prepared baking sheet, or pipe the meringues, using a piping bag fitted with a 1.5cm fluted nozzle. Place in the oven immediately and cook for 1 hour 50 minutes.

Leave to cool a little, then transfer to a wire rack and leave to cool completely in a dry place.

almond-topped meringues Just before these meringues go into the oven, you can sprinkle them with flaked almonds if you like.

chocolate meringues Replace 30g of the sugar with 30g dark, bitter cocoa powder, sifting in the cocoa about a minute before the end of beating.

coffee meringues Carefully fold 2–3 tsp coffee essence or cooled very strong espresso coffee into the whisked meringue.

raspberry (or lemon) meringues Carefully fold a few drops of raspberry (or lemon) essence to taste into the whisked meringue.

petits fours meringues Pipe the meringue (plain or flavoured as above) into little mounds the size of quail's eggs and cook for 30 minutes only.

meringue nests Using a piping bag fitted with a 2cm nozzle, pipe meringue rounds on the prepared baking sheet, 8–10cm in diameter, then pipe an extra ring (or two) of meringue on the edge to form baskets. Bake as for meringues, allowing about 1½ hours. Illustrated on page 139

plum meringues

makes 4 large meringues

These are delicious eaten within 24 hours of making, with the plum juice slightly oozing from them.

300g ripe plums in season (ideally Victoria),
    or greengages or damsons, washed
300ml stock syrup (page 275)
2 bay leaves
1 quantity French meringue mixture (page 146)

Using a small knife, remove the stones from the plums, without cutting them entirely in half. Put the plums into a dish. Heat the stock syrup with the bay leaves in a saucepan over a medium heat. As soon as it reaches the boil, pour the syrup over the plums and set aside to cool completely.

Preheat the oven to 100°C/Gas ¼. Line a baking sheet with baking parchment or a silicone liner. Drain the cooled plums and dab them lightly on kitchen paper to remove as much syrup as possible. Using a large spoon, fold them lightly into the meringue mixture.

Now, using 2 large spoons, take a quarter of the meringue and shape into a large quenelle by passing it between the spoons, then place on the prepared baking sheet. Repeat to make another 3 meringues. Cook in the oven for 2 hours.

Leave the meringues on the baking sheet to cool a little, then use a palette knife to transfer them to a wire rack. Leave in a dry place to cool completely before serving.

You can also make these meringues using fresh cherries –
always a hit with children.

italian meringue

makes about 650g

360g caster sugar
30g liquid glucose (optional)
6 egg whites

Put 80ml water into a heavy-based pan and add the
sugar and glucose, if using. Bring to the boil over a
medium heat, stirring with a skimmer. Skim off any
scum and brush down any crystals forming on the side
of the pan using a brush dipped in cold water. Increase
the heat and put a sugar thermometer in the pan.

When the temperature reaches 110°C, start to beat
the egg whites in a clean bowl, using an electric whisk,
or by hand. Keep an eye on the sugar syrup, and
remove from the heat the moment it reaches 121°C.

When the egg whites form stiff peaks, slowly pour
in the sugar syrup in a thin, steady stream, whisking
constantly as you do so.

Continue beating on a low speed for about
15 minutes, until the mixture has cooled
to about 30°C. It is now ready to use.

Italian meringue mixture, which forms part of other desserts, keeps
perfectly for 2–3 days in the fridge, in an airtight container.

tutti frutti pavlova

serves 10

I have used exotic fruits to top my pavlova here, allowing me to serve it at any time of the year, even in winter, but in summer an assortment of berries is the obvious choice.

1½ quantities French meringue mixture (page 146)
1 ripe dwarf pineapple or ½ regular pineapple
1 ripe mango, about 300g
1 ripe papaya, about 200g

4 ripe kiwi fruit
400ml whipping cream
200g blueberries
6 passion fruit, halved
20 fresh hazelnuts, in season (optional)

Preheat the oven to 150°C/Gas 2. Line a baking tray with a silicone liner or baking parchment. Place a lightly oiled 24cm metal ring, about 7cm deep, on the sheet and fill with the meringue. (Alternatively, draw a 24cm circle on the baking parchment, turn the paper over and spread the meringue within the marked circle.) Very lightly smooth the top, leaving enough texture to achieve a slightly rustic look. Remove the ring, if using, by lifting it and giving it a slight twist as you do so.

Cook in the oven for 30 minutes, then lower the setting to 120°C/Gas ½ and cook for at least another hour. Turn off the oven and leave the pavlova inside to cool slowly for at least 6–8 hours. At this stage, the meringue should be soft in the middle with a crisp exterior, and slightly crackled around the edges.

Using a knife, peel the pineapple, quarter and remove the core. Peel the mango and cut the flesh from the stone. Peel and deseed the papaya. Peel the kiwi fruit. Cut these fruits into slivers, cubes or thin slices. Lightly whip the cream to a ribbon consistency.

Carefully transfer the pavlova to a serving plate. Spread the cream generously over the top and arrange the prepared fruit on the cream. Scatter the blueberries over the surface. Using a teaspoon, scoop the pulp out of the passion fruit and spoon on top of the pavlova. Sprinkle the hazelnuts on top, if using. Serve at once.

illustrated on previous page

serves 6

To warm the meringue, you can brown it in a very hot oven at
250°C/Gas 9 for a minute, instead of using a cook's blowtorch.
This gives a lovely contrast to the frozen ice cream.

1 quantity sponge finger mixture
  (page 279)
500ml crème anglaise (page 56)
1 vanilla pod, split lengthways
1 tbsp instant coffee, dissolved in 1 tbsp
  warm water
3–4 tbsp Grand Marnier (optional)
1 quantity Italian meringue (page 152)

Preheat the oven to 180°C/Gas 4. Spread the sponge mixture in a non-stick loaf tin,
20–22cm long, to two-thirds fill it. Bake for 25 minutes. Leave in the tin for 5 minutes
then turn out onto a wire rack to cool. Cut a 2cm slice off the top for the 'lid'. Using a
knife and a spoon, hollow out the inside of the sponge to create a large cavity.

For the ice creams, divide the crème anglaise between 2 bowls. Scrape the vanilla seeds
into one bowl and whisk to incorporate. Add the coffee to the second bowl, whisking
to mix well. Churn the vanilla ice cream in an ice-cream machine for 15–20 minutes,
then freeze in a suitable container. Repeat to make the coffee ice cream.

If using the Grand Marnier, brush over the hollowed-out inside of the sponge and
over the lid. Place the sponge base on a large piece of cling film and fill with alternate
scoops of vanilla and coffee ice cream, so that the ice cream comes at least 2–3cm
above the top of the sponge. Put the lid on top, then bring up the sides of the cling film
and wrap the whole dessert. Place in the freezer for 1–2 hours.

To serve, remove the cling film and place the dessert on a heatproof serving tray. Put
the meringue into a piping bag fitted with a 1.5–2cm fluted nozzle and pipe over the
top and sides of the dessert to cover it completely. With a cook's blowtorch, lightly
brown the meringue all over. Serve at once, cutting the baked alaska into slices with
a very sharp knife dipped in hot water between each slice.

meringue and red berry layers

serves 6

The meringue, fruit and coulis can all be prepared a day ahead,
ready to assemble quickly as you are about to serve. For total indulgence,
serve with a scoop of vanilla ice cream (page 126).

1 quantity French meringue mixture (page 146)
50g flaked almonds, lightly toasted
400ml stock syrup (page 275)
500g ripe mixed red berries in season, washed
  and de-stalked (little gariguette or similar
  strawberries, redcurrants, white currants,
  blueberries, raspberries, wild strawberries etc.)
juice of 1 lemon

Preheat the oven to 100°C/Gas ¼. Draw 9 circles, 7–8cm in diameter, on each of
2 large baking sheets lined with baking parchment and invert the paper. Using a
palette knife, spread a 4mm layer of meringue over each marked circle and smooth
with a palette knife. Sprinkle all the rounds with the flaked almonds. Cook in the
oven for 1 hour, then set aside to cool. When cold, carefully remove from the baking
parchment and leave in a dry place until ready to assemble.

Bring the stock syrup to the boil in a pan, then reduce to a simmer. Put the firmer
fruits in first, then every 30 seconds add another variety, finishing with the wild
strawberries. Immediately remove from the heat and leave to cool. Carefully drain
the fruits over another pan to collect the syrup.

Take about a fifth of the least shapely poached fruits and add to the stock syrup.
Cook over a medium heat for 10 minutes, then tip into a blender. Add the lemon juice
and blend for 30 seconds, then strain through a fine sieve. Set this coulis aside.

Place a meringue round on each serving plate. Carefully spoon some of the poached
fruits onto each meringue and coat with a little of the coulis. Cover with another
meringue round and spoon on the remaining fruits. Coat with more coulis, then top
with a final meringue round. Spoon more coulis around the plate. Serve at once.

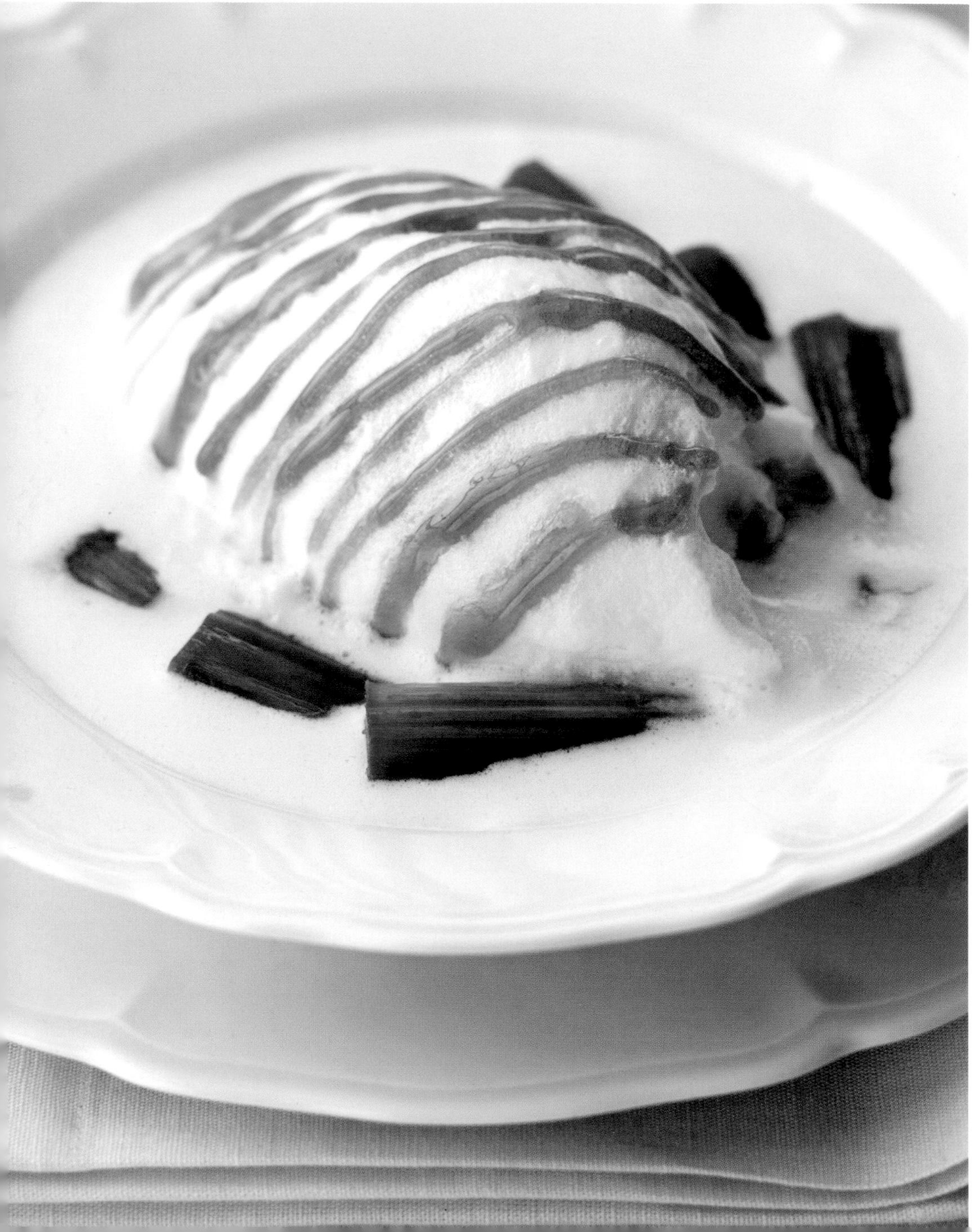

serves 4

I like my rhubarb a tiny bit on the crunchy side, but if you
prefer it to be softer, simply poach it in the syrup for 5 minutes.

2 young, tender rhubarb stalks
1 litre milk
190g caster sugar
6 egg whites
250ml crème anglaise (page 56)

syrup
150g caster sugar

caramel
210g caster sugar

Peel the rhubarb, if necessary, then rinse and cut into 5cm long batons, 2cm wide.
Place in a dish. For the syrup, dissolve the sugar in 250ml water in a saucepan over a
medium heat and bring to the boil. Immediately pour over the rhubarb and set aside.

Put the milk and 60g of the sugar in a sauté pan, heat to about 85°C and lower the
heat to maintain this temperature. Beat the egg whites using an electric whisk to
firm peaks, then beat in the remaining sugar; the meringue should hold stiff peaks.

Using a large serving spoon, scoop out a quenelle of meringue and smooth it using
a palette knife. Dip the quenelle into the hot milk; the quenelle will slide off the spoon
into the pan. Rinse the spoon in cold water, then repeat to make 4 quenelles in total.
Poach in the milk for 2 minutes, then turn carefully, using a slotted spoon, and poach
for 2 minutes more. Carefully lift out the quenelles and lay on a clean tea towel.

For the caramel, melt the sugar in a small pan over a low heat. As soon as the syrup
turns a light golden caramel colour, remove from the heat.

Divide the crème anglaise between 4 shallow bowls. Use a palette knife to transfer
a quenelle to each bowl. Drain the rhubarb and arrange around the 'islands'. Drizzle
the caramel decoratively over the 'islands'. Leave for 5 minutes before serving.

genoese

makes a 20cm sponge cake

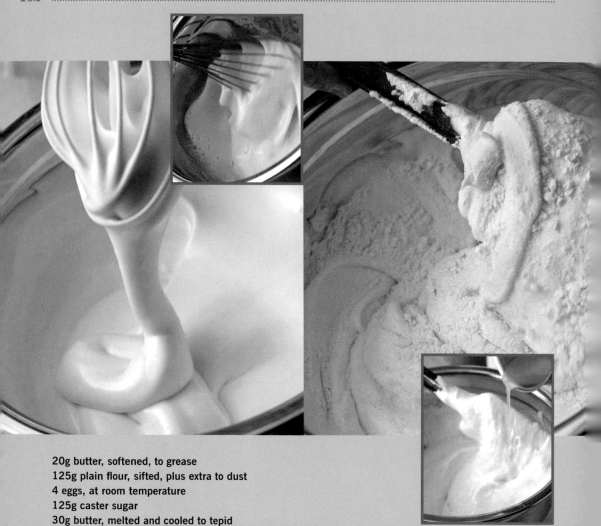

20g butter, softened, to grease
125g plain flour, sifted, plus extra to dust
4 eggs, at room temperature
125g caster sugar
30g butter, melted and cooled to tepid

Preheat the oven to 190°C/Gas 5. Butter and lightly flour a 20cm loose-based cake tin. Whisk the eggs and sugar together in a bowl.

Continue to whisk for about 12 minutes, until the mixture leaves a ribbon trail when you lift the whisk. (You can also do this in an electric mixer.)

Shower in the flour and delicately fold it into the mixture, with a rubber spatula.

Add the melted butter and fold in carefully, without overworking the mixture.

Pour the mixture into the prepared tin and bake for
30 minutes, or until lightly springy to the touch.
Invert on to a wire rack to cool, giving the sponge
a quarter-turn after 10 minutes to stop it sticking.
For a simple dessert, once cold, split horizontally
into two layers and fill with whipped cream and
soft fruits, moistened with a little redcurrant coulis
(page 20). Dust with icing sugar to serve.

For a chocolate Genoese,
replace 50g of the plain flour
with good-quality cocoa powder.

mango charlotte

serves 8–10

illustrated on previous page

1 quantity sponge finger mixture
  (page 279)
about 100g icing sugar, sifted
200ml whipping cream
120g Italian meringue mixture (page 152)
100g mango flesh, cut into small dice

mango crème anglaise
35ml milk
200ml finely sieved mango purée
juice of ½ lime
3 egg yolks
20g caster sugar
1½ sheets leaf gelatine

to finish
½ mango, peeled and sliced into thin strips
16 perfect raspberries
300ml raspberry coulis (page 21)
icing sugar, to dust

Preheat the oven to 220°C/Gas 7. Line a 40x60cm baking sheet with a silicone liner or baking parchment. Put the sponge finger mixture into a piping bag fitted with a 1.5cm plain nozzle. Pipe parallel straight lines, about 8cm long, down one side of the baking sheet, leaving about 5mm between each, to make a complete row, then do the same on the other side of the baking sheet. As they cook, the biscuits will spread very slightly so that they just join up and form 2 strips (as shown on page 164). Immediately dust generously with icing sugar. Leave to stand for 5 minutes.

Give the sponge fingers a second, lighter dusting (for a pearly beading effect) and bake for 8 minutes, until golden. Leave on the baking sheet for 1 minute, then invert both strips onto a tea towel placed on a wire rack and peel off the lining. Set aside to cool.

For the crème anglaise, put the milk, mango purée and lime juice into a saucepan and bring slowly to the boil. Whisk the egg yolks and sugar together in a bowl, almost to a ribbon consistency. Meanwhile, soften the gelatine in cold water to cover for 5 minutes. As soon as the milk mixture comes to the boil, pour it onto the egg yolks, whisking as you do so, then pour the mixture back into the pan. Cook over a low heat, stirring all the time, until the custard coats the back of a spoon and reaches 83°C. Strain through a fine sieve or chinois into a bowl. Drain the gelatine and squeeze out excess water, then add to the custard, stirring to dissolve. Allow to cool, to about 10–15°C.

This is such a lovely dessert and it freezes well wrapped in cling film, so my advice is to double the quantities and make two – one for another occasion. Don't attempt to reduce the quantities to make a smaller charlotte; the recipe won't be successful.

Any leftover biscuit trimmings can be cut into cubes and served in individual bowls at teatime, topped with chocolate sauce (page 274).

Using a serrated knife, trim one long side of one of the biscuit strips, to make a straight edge. From the other strip, cut out 2 circles, 14cm in diameter. Line the inside of a 16cm diameter, 7cm high ring with the trimmed strip of biscuit, with the beaded side facing out and the trimmed edge on the bottom. Trim away any biscuit fingers that form an overlap where the edges meet, to create a seamless band inside the ring. Place the biscuit-lined ring on a board. Put one of the biscuit rounds into the bottom of the ring, to form the base.

In a large bowl, whip the cream to a ribbon consistency. Add the Italian meringue and use a whisk to combine, without overworking. Now fold in the mango crème anglaise, using a rubber spatula, until evenly combined. Incorporate the mango dice, then spoon half of this mixture into the lined ring, on top of the biscuit base. Place the second biscuit round on top, lightly pressing with your fingertips. Pour the remaining mango mixture on top of this biscuit layer, to come 1cm below the crested biscuit rim. Refrigerate for 4 hours, or place in the freezer for 2 hours.

To serve, carefully transfer the charlotte to a serving plate. Gently lift off the ring, then arrange the mango strips on top of the charlotte, lightly folding and twisting them to create a decorative finish. Top with the raspberries, very delicately dusted with icing sugar. Serve the coulis in a jug on the side.

roulé marquis

serves 6–8

3 egg yolks
175g icing sugar, plus extra to dust
4 egg whites
50g good-quality dark, bitter cocoa powder
15g potato flour
20g butter, softened, to grease
30g plain flour, to dust
250ml whipping cream
250ml raspberry coulis (page 21)
150g raspberries

Using an electric whisk, beat the egg yolks and 80g of the icing sugar in a bowl to a ribbon consistency. Whisk the egg whites in a separate clean bowl to soft peaks, then add 45g of the icing sugar and whisk to firm peaks. Using a whisk, incorporate one-third of the egg whites into the egg yolks, then fold in the remaining whites with a metal spoon. Before it is completely mixed, sift the cocoa and potato flour over the mixture and fold in gently; don't overwork it, or the mixture will lose its lightness.

Preheat the oven to 200°C/Gas 6. Line a baking tray with lightly buttered and floured baking parchment or a silicone liner. Using a palette knife, spread the mixture on the lined tray, to a rectangle, about 26x30cm and 1.5cm thick. Cook in the oven for 8–10 minutes. To check to see if it is done, lightly press the middle of the roulade with your fingertips; it should feel slightly springy and lightly resistant.

Turn the roulade out onto a wire rack lined with a tea towel. After a minute, carefully remove the parchment or liner. Set aside in a cool place for 5 minutes. Meanwhile, whip the cream with the remaining 50g icing sugar to a ribbon consistency.

Slide the roulade from the rack onto a sheet of greaseproof paper. Using a brush, spread a quarter of the fruit coulis over the roulade, then use a serrated knife to trim the edges (which will be slightly dry) from all 4 sides. Using a palette knife, spread the cream over

This is a meltingly soft, light dessert that everyone loves. It can be prepared the day before and stored in the fridge overnight – covered with a clean, light tea towel.

the roulade, leaving a 1.5cm border around the edge. Sprinkle the raspberries over the cream. Gently roll up from a long side, using the greaseproof paper to help you (as shown). Refrigerate the roulé for 2–3 hours.

To serve, cut into slices, place on serving plates and sprinkle with a dusting of icing sugar. Drizzle the rest of the coulis around each slice, or serve it on the side in a jug.

The technical skills involved in this chapter can be off-putting and cause people to think twice about having a go. This is a great shame, because mousses are so delicious and everyone loves them. Indeed, if you use a fruit purée or chocolate as a base, a mousse is relatively straightforward to prepare. Don't be afraid to tackle a bavarois either: the step-by-step guide (on pages 192–4) takes you through the recipe to a successful result – guaranteed to win accolades from your friends, who will applaud your skill and artistry.

mousses, parfaits & bavarois

raspberry mousse

172

1½ sheets leaf gelatine
300ml raspberry purée (about 400g fruit
   puréed in a blender and sieved)
120g Italian meringue mixture (page 152)
100ml whipping cream
2 tbsp raspberry eau-de-vie or kirsch
18–24 raspberries, to finish

Soak the gelatine in a shallow dish of cold water
to cover to soften for about 5 minutes.

In another bowl, whip the cream to soft peaks.
Using a rubber spatula, gently fold the whipped
cream into the meringue and purée mixture.

Pour the raspberry purée into a bowl and mix in
the Italian meringue, using a balloon whisk.

Warm the eau-de-vie or kirsch in a small pan to
about 50°C. Drain the gelatine, squeeze out excess
water and add to the alcohol off the heat, stirring
to dissolve. Pour into the mousse mixture, folding
it in with the spatula until evenly combined.

Spoon the mousse into 6–8 glasses, depending on size, and refrigerate for at least 2 hours.

An easy dessert, which also works well with strawberries, blackcurrants or blackberries. The eau-de-vie helps to bring out the flavour of the berries, but if the fruit seems to be a little lacking in flavour, add a squeeze of lemon juice to the purée.

To serve, top each mousse with a trio of raspberries. Little madeleines (page 262) are a lovely accompaniment.

lime mousse with wild strawberries

serves 8

1 sheet leaf gelatine
100ml lime juice
45g caster sugar
100g warm Italian meringue mixture (page 152)
170ml whipping cream
10g lime zest julienne
250g hulled wild strawberries

Soften the gelatine in a shallow dish of cold water to cover for about 5 minutes. In a small saucepan, heat half the lime juice with 15g of the sugar until the sugar has dissolved and the lime syrup is hot, then remove from the heat. Immediately drain the gelatine and squeeze out excess water, then add to the lime syrup, stirring until melted. Stir in the rest of the lime juice.

Pour the lime syrup into the meringue and mix it in lightly, using a whisk. In another bowl, whip the cream to a ribbon consistency, then fold into the lime mixture using a spatula or large metal spoon. Divide between 8 glasses and refrigerate.

In a small saucepan, dissolve the remaining 30g sugar in 6 tbsp water and bring gently to the boil. Add the lime zest julienne and simmer for 1 minute, stirring with a fork, then drain the zest and set aside.

To serve, neatly pile the strawberries on top of each lime mousse and arrange the zest julienne on top. Serve lightly chilled, not too cold.

Any delicate berries can be used instead of wild strawberries – try gariguette strawberries or raspberries. This dessert can be made a day ahead.

serves 4–6

White chocolate marries beautifully with kaffir lime, but if you can't find the fresh fruit, you could use kaffir lime leaves instead of zest, infusing 2 or 3 leaves in the hot milk and removing before adding the gelatine.

150g white chocolate couverture (preferably
   Valrhona), finely chopped
½ sheet leaf gelatine
50ml milk
finely grated zest of 1 (washed) kaffir lime

1½ tsp liquid glucose
2 egg yolks
150ml whipping cream
30g icing sugar

Set a heatproof bowl over a saucepan, one-third filled with hot water, making sure the bowl is not in direct contact with the water. Add the white chocolate to the bowl and place the saucepan over a very low heat. As soon as the chocolate is semi-melted, remove the bowl from the pan.

Meanwhile, soak the gelatine in a shallow dish of cold water to cover to soften for about 5 minutes. Heat the milk in a small pan, then as soon as it boils, add the kaffir lime zest and remove from the heat. Drain the gelatine, squeeze out excess water and add to the hot milk mixture, stirring to dissolve. Set aside to infuse for 3 minutes.

In a separate bowl, mix the glucose, 1 tbsp warm water and the egg yolks together until evenly combined. In a third bowl, whip the cream together with the icing sugar to a ribbon consistency.

Pour the hot milk mixture over the semi-melted chocolate and mix with a balloon whisk until smooth, without overworking. Now gently fold in the egg yolk mixture until homogenous. Finally, using a spatula, carefully fold in the whipped cream. Pour into 4–6 cups or little dishes, depending on size. Refrigerate for at least an hour.

Serve lightly chilled (not icy-cold) to fully appreciate the flavour. Tuiles (page 269) make a perfect accompaniment.

chocolate mousse, lavender crémeux and berry compote

makes 12

This recipe really isn't suitable to make in small quantities, but the individual desserts freeze very well, for up to 15 days without diminishing at all in quality.

berry compote
200g caster sugar
400g mixed red berries (strawberries, redcurrants, raspberries, blueberries, wild strawberries etc.)
juice of 1 lemon

base
400g chocolate Genoese sponge mixture (page 163)

To make the compote, dissolve the sugar in 200ml water in a saucepan over a medium heat. Bring to the boil, then reduce to a simmer. Now add the berries, one variety after another according to size, ripeness and fragility – strawberries first, wild strawberries last. Poach for about 2 minutes, then leave to cool in the syrup. When cooled, carefully strain the berries. Return the syrup to the pan, let bubble over a brisk heat to reduce by two-thirds, then pour over the berries. Add the lemon juice, cover and refrigerate.

For the sponge base, preheat the oven to 180°C/Gas 4. Lay a 40x60cm piece of baking parchment on a baking sheet. Using a palette knife, spread the chocolate sponge mixture evenly over the parchment. Bake for 5–6 minutes, then slide the parchment and sponge onto a wire rack and set aside to cool. Once cooled, cut out 12 rounds from the sponge, using 6.5cm metal rings, 3.5cm high, leaving the sponge circles in the rings. Carefully transfer the rings with the sponge bases to a tray.

To make the lavender crémeux, lightly mix the egg yolks and sugar together, using a small whisk. Put the single cream and lavender flowers in a saucepan and slowly heat to simmering point, then pour onto the egg and sugar mix, stirring with the whisk as you do so. Pour back into the saucepan and cook over a gentle heat until slightly thickened, stirring very lightly and taking care not to let the mixture go above 85°C.

illustrated on previous page

Frosted young lavender stems, when available, are a lovely finish for this (as shown). Simply brush with a little egg white, then sprinkle with caster sugar and leave to dry for several hours in a warm place (at 24–30°C) before using.

crémeux
3 egg yolks
40g caster sugar
250ml single cream
3g lavender flowers (not in full blossom)
1 sheet leaf gelatine

chocolate mousse
200g good-quality dark chocolate,
   70% cocoa solids (preferably Valrhona),
   chopped into small pieces
150ml crème anglaise (page 56)
240ml double cream

Meanwhile, soften the gelatine in a shallow dish of cold water to cover for about 5 minutes. Remove the crémeux from the heat. Drain the gelatine, squeeze out excess water and add to the crémeux, stirring to dissolve. Strain through a fine sieve or chinois, then process in a blender or food processor for 30 seconds. Transfer to a bowl and leave to cool, giving it a brief stir from time to time, then refrigerate to firm up.

To make the mousse, put the chocolate into a bowl. Gently heat the crème anglaise and pour over the chocolate, stirring, then use a balloon whisk to mix until melted and smooth. In another bowl, whip the cream to a ribbon consistency, then gently fold into the mousse, using a rubber spatula, so you aerate the mousse without overworking it.

As soon as the crémeux has firmed up, put it into a piping bag fitted with a 1cm plain nozzle and pipe mounds, 2cm in diameter, centrally on the sponge rounds in the rings. Chill for 10 minutes, until set. Spoon the chocolate mousse into the rings, filling them to the top and enclosing the crémeux. Tap each lightly to eliminate any air bubbles and gently smooth the surface with a palette knife. Refrigerate until ready to serve.

To unmould each dessert, use a cook's blowtorch or a hot tea towel to briefly heat the outside of the ring, then lift it off, pushing the sponge gently up from underneath as you do so. Place on a plate with a generous spoonful of berry compote alongside. Serve immediately.

fromage blanc mousses with thyme-poached peaches

makes 12

base
1 Joconde sponge, 40x60cm (page 276)

mousse
2 egg yolks
50ml sweet white wine
20g caster sugar
2 sheets leaf gelatine
225g creamy fromage blanc (20% fat)
40g runny lavender honey
150ml whipping cream

thyme-poached peaches
350g caster sugar
6 fresh thyme sprigs
6 ripe yellow-fleshed peaches

Using 12 metal 8x4cm rectangular moulds or 6.5cm metal rings, 3cm high, cut out 12 sponge bases. Place the moulds, with the sponge inside, on a baking tray.

Put the egg yolks, wine and sugar into a heatproof bowl, set over a pan of simmering water and whisk for 5–6 minutes, until the mixture reaches a thick ribbon consistency (at 55–60°C). Remove from the heat. Soften the gelatine in a shallow dish of cold water to cover for about 5 minutes. Put the fromage blanc into a large bowl.

Heat the honey in a small pan, then take off the heat. Drain the gelatine, squeeze out excess water and add to the honey, stirring to dissolve. Pour this onto the fromage blanc, whisking vigorously. Using a rubber spatula, fold in the barely warm whisked mixture. In another bowl, whip the cream to a ribbon consistency, then fold into the mousse mixture. Fill the moulds with the mousse. Refrigerate for at least 6 hours.

For the thyme-poached peaches, bring 1 litre water to the boil in a saucepan with the sugar and thyme sprigs added. Lower the heat to a simmer. To peel the peaches, lightly run a knife tip around the circumference and plunge into a pan of boiling water. As soon as the skin starts to lift, take out and refresh in a bowl of iced water. Remove and peel away the skins, then plunge the peaches into the thyme syrup and simmer for 2–3 minutes. Let the peaches cool in the syrup slightly, then take out and cut the flesh into small dice. Place in a bowl, pour on some of the syrup and let cool, then chill.

Perfect for a summer party, this dessert can be prepared a few days ahead and kept in the fridge. It isn't a recipe that can be scaled down successfully.

To unmould each dessert, use a cook's blowtorch or hot tea towel to briefly heat the outside of the mould, then lift it off, pushing the sponge up from underneath gently as you do so. Place on a plate.

Spoon the syrupy peach dice over and around the mousses and decorate each with a thyme sprig from the syrup. Serve at once.

apricot and cognac mousse with caramelised almonds

serves 6–8

For this elegant and delicate dessert, the crunch of the almond caramel coating contrasts beautifully with the silkiness of the apricot mousse.

850ml stock syrup (page 275)
1 vanilla pod, split lengthways
10 ripe apricots
2 sheets leaf gelatine
30ml Cognac
250ml very cold double cream

caramelised almonds
125g caster sugar
40g liquid glucose
32 blanched almonds

Put 750ml of the stock syrup and the vanilla pod into a medium saucepan and bring to the boil. Add the apricots and simmer gently for 3–5 minutes, depending on ripeness, then leave the fruit to cool in the syrup. Chill the remaining 100ml syrup.

For the almonds, put 50ml water into a small pan, add the sugar and bring slowly to the boil. Add the glucose and heat to 155°C, then take off the heat. One at a time, spear the almonds onto a cocktail stick and dip in the syrup, then lift out and hold over the pan to drain until an elongated drip forms and slightly hardens. Transfer to a lightly oiled baking sheet, remove the cocktail stick and set aside in a dry place.

For the mousse, soften the gelatine in cold water to cover for about 5 minutes. Drain the apricots, halve and remove the stones. Set aside 6–8 perfect apricot halves for decoration. Purée the rest in a food processor until smooth. If necessary, pass through a sieve. Heat the Cognac in a small pan for a few seconds, then remove. Drain the gelatine and squeeze out excess water, then add to the Cognac, stirring to dissolve.

Whip the cream with the chilled syrup to a ribbon consistency, then fold in the apricot purée and gelatine mixture. Divide between 6–8 glasses and chill for at least 4 hours.

To serve, place a reserved apricot half on each mousse, and surround with a few caramelised almonds, placing one at the base of the glass. Serve at once.

chilled limoncello parfait with raspberries

makes 12

A lovely party dessert. It isn't practicable to make a smaller quantity, but you can always freeze parfaits you do not need to serve straight away.

1 large egg, plus 5 egg yolks
100g caster sugar
finely grated zest of 2 lemons
25ml lemon juice (2–3 lemons)
½ sheet leaf gelatine
60ml limoncello liqueur
150ml whipping cream
150ml double cream

raspberry topping
500g raspberries
100g caster sugar
12–14 mint sprigs

Mix the egg, egg yolks, sugar, lemon zest and juice in a heatproof bowl, then set over a pan of simmering water (the bowl must not touch the water). Whisk until the mixture reaches 80–85°C. Take the bowl off the pan and continue to whisk until the mixture cools to 20–25°C, about 10 minutes. Meanwhile, soak the gelatine in cold water to cover.

Heat one-third of the limoncello in a small pan, then remove from the heat. Drain the gelatine, squeeze out excess water and add to the hot limoncello, stirring to dissolve. Let cool slightly, then mix in the remaining limoncello. Lightly whisk this into the cooled lemon mixture. In a separate bowl, whip the creams together to a ribbon consistency, then fold into the lemon mixture, using a rubber spatula.

Place 12 metal 5cm rings, 3.5cm high, on a tray and fill with the parfait mixture. Place in the freezer for at least 2–3 hours. Meanwhile, for the topping, select 150g of the most perfect raspberries, halve them and set aside. Purée the remaining berries with the sugar in a blender or food processor for 1 minute, then pass through a fine sieve or chinois into a bowl. Cover and refrigerate.

To unmould the parfaits, one at a time, briefly warm the outside of the ring using a cook's blowtorch or hot tea towel and release the parfait onto a serving plate. Using a teaspoon dipped in hot water, scoop out a little from the middle of each one, making a hollow. Fill with the raspberries, spoon on some coulis, add a mint sprig and serve.

nougat glacé with roasted figs

serves 6–8

A richly flavoured, meltingly smooth dessert, with a hint of crunch from
the almond and pistachio nougatine.

6 small, ripe green or black figs
120g caster sugar
30g pistachio nuts, lightly roasted
60g flaked almonds, lightly roasted
1–2 tsp groundnut oil, to oil
60g runny honey
15g liquid glucose
3 egg whites
140ml double cream
60g mixed glacé fruits (pineapple, cherries etc.),
   cut into small dice

Preheat the oven to 170°C/Gas 3. Stand the figs in a small roasting dish, sprinkle with
30g sugar and roast for 20–30 minutes until tender. Transfer to a plate, with any juices.

Melt 60g sugar in a small heavy-based saucepan over a low heat, stirring. As soon as
the syrup turns light caramel in colour, add the nuts and cook, stirring, for 1 minute.
Tip onto a lightly oiled baking sheet and leave to cool and harden, about 30 minutes.
Transfer the nougatine to a board and use a rolling pin to roughly break it up.

Melt the remaining 30g sugar with the honey and glucose in a small heavy-based pan
over a low heat, then turn up the heat slightly and heat until the syrup registers 110°C
on a sugar thermometer. Meanwhile, whisk the egg whites in a clean bowl to firm peaks.
Once at the desired temperature, pour the syrup onto the egg whites in a steady stream,
whisking constantly. Continue to whisk until the meringue is cooled to 35°C.

Whip the cream to a ribbon consistency, then fold in the meringue followed by the glacé
fruits, then the nougatine. Place 6–8 moulds or metal rings, 8cm in diameter and 3cm
tall on a tray. Divide the mixture between them. Place in the freezer for at least 2 hours.

To unmould, briefly dip the moulds in hot water or use a cook's blowtorch to warm
the outside of the metal rings, and release each nougat onto a serving plate. Place a
cooled, roasted fig on each and pour on a little of the fig cooking juices. Serve at once.

Anise is one of my favourite parfait flavours and the blackberry coulis complements it beautifully. You can make the parfait several days in advance; it keeps well in the freezer.

1 egg, plus 3 egg yolks
50g caster sugar
100ml whipping cream
100ml double cream
30ml Ricard or Pernod

to serve
200ml blackberry coulis (page 21)
handful of blackberries

Put the egg, egg yolks and sugar into a small heatproof bowl. Stand the bowl over a small saucepan one-third filled with hot water at 50–60°C (the bowl must not touch the water) and place over a gentle heat. Whisk the mixture, using a balloon whisk, until it reaches a ribbon consistency. Remove the bowl from the pan and continue to whisk until the mixture has cooled noticeably, to 25–30°C.

In another bowl, whip the creams together with the Ricard or Pernod to a ribbon consistency. Fold into the whisked egg and sugar mixture, using a rubber spatula, without overworking the mixture.

Place 8 metal rings, 7cm in diameter, on a baking sheet or tray lined with greaseproof paper, and divide the parfait mixture between them. Cover with cling film and freeze until ready to serve.

To unmould the parfaits, one at a time, briefly warm the outside of the ring using a cook's blowtorch or hot tea towel and release the parfait onto a serving plate. Surround with a little blackberry coulis and arrange a few blackberries on the side.

macaroons filled with parfait à l'anis

serves 8

A very special dessert. You can make the parfait, macaroons and coulis a day or two ahead, ready to assemble just before serving.

parfait
1 quantity anise parfait mixture (page 189)

macaroons
185g caster sugar
150ml egg whites (about 5 medium)
190g ground almonds
190g icing sugar
1–2 knife tips of yellow food colouring powder

to assemble
about 6 oven-dried blackberries, crushed
(page 16)
200ml blackberry coulis (page 21)
12 fresh blackberries, halved

Place 8 metal 7cm rings on a tray lined with greaseproof paper, divide the parfait mixture between them and cover with cling film. Freeze until ready to assemble.

For the macaroons, dissolve 170g sugar in 50ml water in a small pan over a low heat. Meanwhile, in a heatproof bowl, whisk 70ml egg whites until firm, then whisk in the remaining 15g sugar a little at a time, until very firm. Still whisking but slowly, pour in the hot sugar syrup (it should be at 110°C), then continue to whisk slowly until the mixture has almost cooled and is at about 40°C.

Sift the ground almonds and icing sugar together into a large bowl. Mix the remaining 80ml egg whites with the colouring powder, then add to the almond mixture and mix to a semi-firm paste. Now, using a rubber spatula, incorporate the meringue, until the mixture is firm and glossy. Using a piping bag fitted with a 1cm plain nozzle, pipe 16 discs, 6cm in diameter, onto a baking sheet lined with baking parchment, spacing them 3cm apart. Leave for 20 minutes. Preheat the oven to 150°C/Gas 2.

Sprinkle just a little crushed blackberry over each macaroon and bake for 14 minutes. Leave on the baking sheet for 2 minutes, then slide the parchment onto a wire rack and leave for 5–10 minutes before lifting off the macaroons.

Unmould the parfaits onto a tray and leave for 3 minutes, until partially defrosted.

Using a 2cm pastry cutter, cut a circle from the centre of each parfait to make a cavity. Place a parfait on the flat side of half of the macaroons, in the centre. Fill the cavity with a little blackberry coulis. Place the remaining macaroon halves on top, rounded side up.

Serve as shown, with a few berries on the side and a little blackberry coulis spooned around.

mango bavarois

serves 6–8

35ml milk
200ml sieved mango purée
juice of ½ lime
1½ sheets leaf gelatine
3 egg yolks

20g caster sugar
200ml whipping cream
120g Italian meringue mixture (page 152)
1 hazelnut dacquoise (page 277)
1 mango, to decorate (optional)

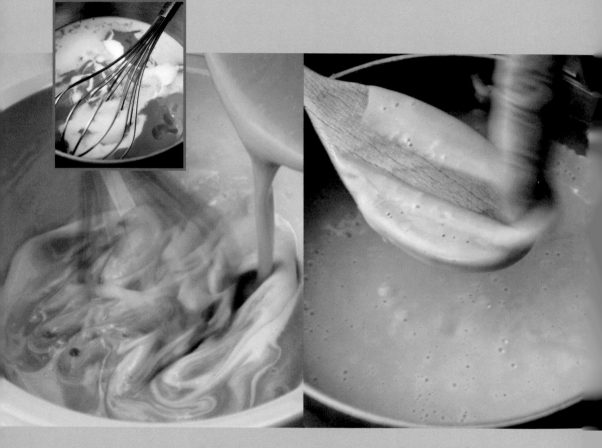

Heat the milk, mango purée and lime juice in a saucepan, stirring occasionally. Meanwhile, soak the gelatine in cold water to cover for about 5 minutes. Whisk the egg yolks and sugar together in a bowl until thick. As the mango mixture comes to the boil, pour it onto the yolks, stirring with a whisk.

Pour the mixture back into the pan and cook gently (at about 80–85°C), stirring until the custard thickens enough to coat the back of the spoon; do not allow to boil. To check that it is thick enough, run your finger down the back of the spoon; it should leave a clear trace.

These keep very well in the freezer for 2 weeks, individually wrapped in cling film. Simply take them out the day before and put them in the fridge a few hours before serving.

Strain the mixture through a fine chinois or sieve into a bowl.

Drain the gelatine, squeeze to remove excess water, then add to the hot mango crème anglaise, stirring to dissolve. Set aside to cool down, stirring occasionally.

In another large bowl, whip the cream to a ribbon consistency. Using a rubber spatula, fold in the Italian meringue followed by the mango crème anglaise.

continued overleaf

Divide the mixture between 6–8 dariole moulds, measuring about 8cm across the top, 5cm across the base and about 5cm high.

Cut discs from the hazelnut dacquoise the same diameter as the top of the moulds. Place a disc on top of each bavarois, pressing it down very lightly with your fingertips. Place in the fridge for 4 hours, or in the freezer for 2 hours.

To unmould the bavarois, briefly dip the moulds halfway in very hot water, then turn them out onto serving plates. Decorate with fine ribbons of mango, cut from the peeled fruit with a very sharp knife, if you like. Serve at once.

raspberry bavarois Blend 220g raspberries in a food processor or blender, then strain through a fine sieve or chinois, to give 200ml purée. Proceed exactly as for the mango bavarois, adding the raspberry purée in place of the mango. To finish, top the bavarois with a few raspberries and dust with icing sugar. Serves 6–8

pear bavarois In a food processor or blender, blend 250g peeled, cored pears with the juice of 1 lemon, then strain through a fine sieve or chinois, to give about 200ml pear purée. Proceed exactly as for the mango bavarois, adding the pear purée in place of the mango, but use an extra ½ leaf gelatine, i.e. 2 leaves in total (as pear is more liquid than mango). To finish, top the bavarois with some diced fresh pear lightly sprinkled with lemon juice and drizzle with a thread of runny honey. Serves 6–8

caramel bavarois with saffron-roasted apples

serves 8 illustrated on previous page

to line the moulds
1 quantity sponge finger mixture
   (page 279)
about 100g icing sugar, sifted

dried apple
120g caster sugar
pinch of saffron strands
1 sharp eating apple, such as Cox, unpeeled

roasted apples
300g sharp eating apples, such as Cox
60g soft brown sugar
generous pinch of saffron strands (1g)

Preheat the oven to 220°C/Gas 7. Line two large baking sheets with a silicone liner or baking parchment. Using a piping bag fitted with an 8mm nozzle, pipe the sponge finger mixture in parallel diagonal lines, 5mm apart, to form a strip, 20cm long and 4cm wide. Repeat to make another 7 strips of the same dimensions. Dust generously with icing sugar and leave to stand for 5 minutes. Dust again with icing sugar and bake for 8 minutes, until golden. Leave on the baking sheets for a minute, then invert the strips onto wire racks lined with tea towels and remove the paper. Leave to cool.

For the dried apple, dissolve the sugar in 250ml water in a pan over a medium heat. Bring to the boil, add the saffron, then set aside to cool. Cut the apples horizontally into wafer-thin slices. Place in a shallow dish, pour on the cold syrup and leave to macerate for 2 hours. Heat the oven to 90°C/Gas ¼. Drain the apple rounds and place on a baking sheet lined with a silicone liner or baking parchment, making sure they are not touching. Dry in the oven for 1 hour 20 minutes. Set aside in a dry place.

For the roasted apples, heat the oven to 250°C/Gas 9. Peel and core the apples and cut into 2cm cubes. Put into a bowl with the sugar and saffron and toss to mix. Leave for 10 minutes, to allow the sugar to melt. Spread the apple dice out on a baking sheet lined with greaseproof paper and bake for 8–10 minutes until caramelised, turning them with a palette knife every 3 minutes. Set aside to cool on the baking sheet.

For this impressive dessert, the sponge finger strips and dried apple can both be prepared a day or two in advance.

bavarois
2 sheets leaf gelatine
70g caster sugar
120ml milk
290ml whipping cream
2 egg yolks

to serve (optional)
150ml orange butter sauce (page 274)

Line the inside of 8 metal rings, 6.5cm in diameter and 3.5cm tall, with the sponge finger strips, trimming them so they join neatly where the two ends meet, with no overlap. Place on a tray lined with greaseproof paper and refrigerate.

For the bavarois, soak the gelatine in cold water to cover for 5 minutes. Melt 50g of the sugar in a small pan over a low heat, stirring with a wooden spoon. As soon as it forms a dark caramel, add the milk and 120ml cream, then remove from the heat. Whisk the egg yolks and remaining 20g sugar together in a bowl for 1 minute, then pour in the caramel mixture, stirring constantly. Pour back into the pan and cook over a gentle heat as for a crème anglaise, at 84°C, to thicken, stirring all the time. Take off the heat.

Immediately drain the gelatine, squeeze out excess water, add to the crème anglaise and stir until melted. Strain through a chinois or fine sieve into a bowl. Cool quickly over a larger bowl filled with ice, stirring occasionally. Whip the remaining 170ml cream to a ribbon consistency. As soon as the bavarois mixture begins to thicken, fold in the cream, using a rubber spatula, until smoothly incorporated. Fill the biscuit-lined rings with the bavarois. Place in the fridge for 4 hours, or the freezer for 1½ hours to set.

When ready to serve, place a bavarois on each plate and remove the metal ring. Spoon the caramelised apple dice on top, with a dried apple round positioned vertically to one side. Pour a little orange sauce, if using, around each bavarois and serve.

Tarts are excellent all-year-round desserts – a lovely showcase for fruit in season. Simply poach or lightly roast the fruits first, unless they are fragile, in which case you will be able to use them just as they are. To enjoy a tart at its best, serve it warm or cold, but never chilled. For almost all of the recipes in this chapter I have used either pâte sablée or my quick puff pastry, which are both easy to prepare. Maple sweet potato pie and kataifi are treasured recipes that I have acquired on my travels – I urge you to try them. And, for a special occasion, impress your guests with my mini croquembouche.

tarts & pastries

tarte fine au citron

butter, to grease
350g pâte sablée (page 281)
5 eggs
180g caster sugar
150ml double cream
finely grated zest and strained juice
   of 2 lemons
1 egg yolk mixed with 1 tsp milk, to glaze

Lightly butter a 22cm tart tin, about 2cm deep, and chill on a baking tray. Roll out the pastry to a round, 3–4mm thick. Drape it over the rolling pin and unfurl over the tart tin.

Line the tin with the pastry, gently tapping it in with a knob of pastry. Trim off the excess pastry around the rim then, using your index finger and thumb, gently press the pastry edges up the side of the tin to form a fluted lip, about 2mm. Refrigerate for 20 minutes.

Preheat the oven to 190°C/Gas 5. For the filling, lightly whisk the eggs and sugar in a bowl, without letting the mixture turn pale. In another, chilled, bowl, whisk the cream for a few seconds, then mix it into the eggs. Add the lemon zest and juice, stir briefly, cover with cling film and refrigerate.

Line the chilled pastry case with greaseproof paper, fill with baking beans and bake 'blind' for 15 minutes. Remove the beans and paper, leave for a couple of minutes, then brush the base and sides of the pastry with the egg glaze. Bake for a further 5 minutes, until lightly coloured. Take out and lower the temperature to 150°C/Gas 2.

This tart improves on standing, so make it a day in advance and keep it in a cool place, but not the fridge otherwise the pastry will go soggy.

Lightly whisk the chilled lemon filling, then pour it into the tart case up to the level of the lip. Immediately bake for about 1 hour, until lightly set. Leave for about 5 minutes, then carefully remove the tart from the tin. Leave to cool on a wire rack for at least 4 hours before serving.

Serve the tart as it is, or sprinkled with a generous layer of icing sugar. It is delicious accompanied by red berries in season.

basil-scented tarte au citron Add 50g roughly chopped basil leaves to the lemon filling. Cover and refrigerate for at least 6 hours to allow the flavour to infuse. Pass the mixture through a fine sieve or chinois before pouring into the blind-baked pastry case and baking as directed. To finish, brush a few basil leaves with lightly beaten egg white, sprinkle with caster sugar and set aside to dry for a few hours. Decorate the tart with the frosted basil leaves.

Strawberry tart Bake the pastry case 'blind', but cook for an extra 10–15 minutes once you have removed the beans and paper, to cook the pastry right through. Allow to cool for 5 minutes, then remove from the tin and leave to cool completely. Halve 500–700g fragrant strawberries, or leave whole if small. Delicately fold 300g crème chantilly (page 272) into 150g crème patissière (page 273) and use to fill the pastry case. Arrange the strawberries on top, dust lightly with icing sugar and serve. Serves 8

Apricot tart Bake the pastry case 'blind' as for tarte au citron, then set aside to cool in the tin. Turn the oven up to 200°C/Gas 6. Spread 450g crème patissière (page 273) evenly in the pastry case. Arrange 15–20 halved and stoned ripe apricots (depending on size) over the crème patissière. Bake in the hot oven for 20 minutes. Meanwhile, dissolve 80g caster sugar in 80ml water in a small saucepan over a low heat, then bring to the boil and let bubble for 5 minutes to make a syrupy glaze. When the tart is ready, let it cool for a minute or two, then remove from the tin and brush the surface with the syrup to glaze. Serves 8

honey-roasted apricots on sablés bretons

serves 8

To fully appreciate the sublime natural flavour of the apricots,
serve this simple dessert slightly warm, rather than cold.
Lavender ice cream is a delightful addition, though you could
serve vanilla ice cream or cream instead.

sablés
150g butter, softened
3 egg yolks
190g plain flour
1½ tsp baking powder
125g caster sugar
½ tsp coarse sea salt

honey-roasted apricots
16 ripe apricots, about 60g each
200g runny lavender honey

to serve (optional)
lavender ice cream (page 129)
10g lavender flowers (not in full blossom)

To make the sablés, mix the butter and egg yolks on a work surface, using your
fingertips, then add the remaining ingredients and work in with your fingers until
the texture is slightly grainy. Knead with the palm of your hand 3 or 4 times until
smooth, then form the sablé dough into a ball, wrap in cling film and refrigerate for
20 minutes. Preheat the oven to 170°C/Gas 3.

On a lightly floured surface, roll the chilled dough into a sausage, about 4cm in
diameter. Cut 16 rounds, each 2cm thick, and lay on a baking sheet (any leftover
dough can be cooked as biscuits). Bake for 12 minutes, then transfer to a wire rack
and leave to cool. Lower the oven temperature by 10°C/ ½ Gas mark.

Put the apricots into a roasting dish just big enough to fit them all, and spoon the
honey all over them to coat. Roast in the oven for 15–20 minutes, depending on
ripeness, basting every 3–4 minutes with the honey in the dish. Set aside to cool
until just warm.

To serve, place 2 sablés on each plate and top each sablé with an apricot. Place
a scoop of lavender ice cream, if using, between the sablés. Coat the apricots with
a touch of the honey from the dish and sprinkle lavender flowers, if using, on top.

pineapple and blackberry torte

serves 8

I like to serve this torte with a grapefruit and ginger sabayon (page 69), which adds yet another dimension to the pineapple and blackberry flavours.

butter, to grease
400g pâte sablée (page 281)
350g caster sugar
8 star anise
1 ripe pineapple, about 2kg
800g blackberries
1 egg yolk mixed with 2 tsp milk, to glaze

Lightly butter a 20cm tart ring, 2.5cm high, and place on a baking sheet. On a lightly floured surface, roll out 300g of the pâte sablée to a round, 3mm thick, and use to line the tart ring. Prick the pastry in 6 places with a fork. Roll out the rest of the pastry to a 22cm circle and place on a baking sheet. Put both pastry rounds in the fridge to rest.

Put 1 litre water, 250g of the sugar and the star anise in a sauté pan and heat gently. Using a serrated knife, peel the pineapple, then split lengthways into quarters and remove the core. Add the pineapple to the sugar syrup in the sauté pan and candy over a gentle heat for 45 minutes. Leave to cool in the syrup. Once cold, remove and finely chop the pineapple; leave to drain in a chinois or sieve. Discard the star anise.

Put the blackberries in a pan with the remaining 100g sugar and cook over a gentle heat for 30 minutes. Transfer to a bowl and leave to cool. The consistency should be of a semi-cooked jam; if necessary drain off some of the liquid, using a fine sieve.

Preheat the oven to 180°C/Gas 4. Put each of the fruit mixtures in a separate piping bag fitted with a 1–1.5cm nozzle. Pipe a double layer of pineapple around the inside edge of the pastry case, then pipe an adjacent double ring of blackberry inside. Repeat with the remaining pineapple, then fill the centre with the rest of the blackberry mixture.

Brush the pastry rim with egg glaze, then cover the pie with the pastry lid. Using your thumb and index finger, press the edges of the pastry together to seal, then flute the edge. Brush the top of the pie with the glaze, then mark a ridged pattern using a fork. Bake for 25 minutes.

Carefully slide the torte onto a wire rack and remove the tart ring. Leave to cool before serving.

maple bourbon sweet potato pie

serves 8

I adore the rich, silky sweetness of this classic pie from the US Deep South.

pastry
200g plain flour
100g butter, diced, slightly softened, plus
   extra to grease
pinch of salt
50ml cold milk
1 egg yolk mixed with 2 tsp milk, to glaze

filling
750g sweet potatoes (about 3), peeled
200ml milk
200ml double cream

1 cinnamon stick, broken into short
   lengths
6 cloves
12 peppercorns, crushed
¼ tsp freshly grated nutmeg
40g butter, melted
250g maple syrup
60ml Bourbon whisky
75g light muscovado sugar
75g caster sugar
pinch of salt
2 eggs, plus 3 egg yolks

For the pastry, heap the flour on a surface, make a well in the centre and add the butter and salt. Work into the flour with your fingertips until lightly sandy in texture, then incorporate the milk to form a dough. Wrap in cling film and chill for 20 minutes or so.

For the filling, cut the sweet potatoes into 2cm dice and put into a pan with the milk and cream. Add the spices, tied together in muslin. Bring slowly to the boil, reduce to a simmer and lay a cartouche (see page 283) on the surface. Simmer for 30 minutes. Cool a little before removing the spice bag. Purée the mixture in a blender or food processor until smooth, then pass through a fine sieve into a bowl. Leave to stand for 10 minutes, then whisk in the remaining ingredients, one by one, without overworking.

Lightly butter a 23cm loose-bottomed tart tin. On a lightly floured surface, roll out the pastry to a round, 2–3mm thick, and use to line the tart tin, pressing it gently into the base and sides. Rest in the fridge for 20 minutes. Preheat the oven to 170°C/Gas 3. Prick the pastry base lightly with a fork and bake 'blind' (see page 283) for 20 minutes. Brush the base with the egg glaze and put back in the oven to dry out for 5 minutes.

Give the filling a quick stir, then pour into the pastry case and bake for 40 minutes. Leave in the tin for 5 minutes before unmoulding the pie and placing it on a wire rack. Leave to cool for at least an hour before serving, with lightly whipped cream.

serves 8

280g pâte sablée (page 281)
200g ripe fresh raspberries (or frozen ones,
  defrosted and well drained), halved if large

ganache
250ml whipping cream
200g good-quality dark chocolate, 70% cocoa solids
  (preferably Valrhona), cut into pieces
25g liquid glucose
50g butter, cut into small pieces

On a lightly floured surface, roll out the pastry to a round, 2–3mm thick, and use to line a 22cm tart ring, 2.5cm high, placed on a baking tray. Chill for 20 minutes.

Preheat the oven to 190°C/Gas 5. Prick the pastry base lightly in a dozen or so places with a fork. Line the pastry case with greaseproof paper, fill with ceramic baking beans and bake 'blind' for 20 minutes. Remove the paper and baking beans, lower the oven setting to 180°C/Gas 4 and bake the pastry case for another 5 minutes. Transfer to a wire rack and leave until cool enough to handle, then lift off the tart ring.

Once cold, arrange the raspberries in the pastry case, pressing them down lightly with your fingertips so that they stick slightly to the base.

For the ganache, slowly bring the cream to the boil in a pan over a medium heat. Remove from the heat and add the chocolate, using a balloon whisk to mix it in, then add the glucose. Once the mixture is smooth, incorporate the butter, a little at a time.

Pour the ganache over the raspberries to fill the pastry case. Leave to cool, then chill the tart in the fridge for at least 2 hours, before serving.

Use a very sharp knife dipped in boiling water to cut the tart carefully into slices, wiping the knife between each slice. Serve cold, but not straight from the fridge.

individual autumn fruit pies

serves 4

6 apples, ideally Cox or Gala
juice of 1 lemon
320g caster sugar
4 cloves
pinch of freshly grated nutmeg

8 ripe plums, ideally Victoria, or damsons
280g blackberries, halved if large
500g rough puff pastry (page 281)
2 egg yolks mixed with 1½ tbsp milk,
  to glaze

Peel the apples and remove the cores using an apple corer, then cut each one into 8 pieces. Place in a saucepan with the lemon juice, 120g of the sugar, the cloves and nutmeg and cook over a high heat for 4–5 minutes, stirring once. The apples will now be semi-cooked. Transfer to a bowl and set aside.

For the plums, put 250ml water and the remaining 200g sugar into a saucepan. Bring to the boil over a medium heat and skim the surface if necessary. Halve or quarter the plums, according to size, remove the stones and immerse the plums in the boiling syrup. Immediately remove from the heat and leave the plums in the syrup to soften in the residual heat.

Put the blackberries into a bowl and pour on enough of the very hot plum syrup to just cover them. Set aside to cool. Once cold, drain the plums and blackberries, saving the syrup. Boil the syrup in a pan over a high heat to reduce to a semi-syrupy consistency, then set aside until nearly cold.

Tip the apples, plums and blackberries into a large dish or bowl, pour the cooled, reduced syrup over them and mix gently. Divide the fruit between 4 individual oval pie dishes, about 14cm long, 10cm wide and 6cm deep.

illustrated on previous page

All the fruits can be cooked the day before, just leaving
you to assemble the pies an hour or two before cooking them.
Crème anglaise (page 56) is the perfect complement.

On a lightly floured surface, roll out one quarter of the rough puff pastry to a 3mm thickness, in an oval shape 2cm bigger all round than the individual pie dish. Brush the rim of one of the pie dishes with egg glaze and lift the pastry oval over the top. Repeat to make another 3 pies. Place in the fridge for 20 minutes before baking to allow the pastry to rest.

Preheat the oven to 180°C/Gas 4. If necessary, trim away any excess pastry hanging over the edges of the pie dishes, using scissors. Brush the pastry lids with egg glaze and, with a small knife, make small parallel indentations around the edge of the pastry for a decorative finish. Cut out leaf shapes from the pastry trimmings, place these on top of the pies and brush with glaze.

With the point of a knife, make a small hole in the middle of each pie. Bake in the oven for 25 minutes, until the pastry is golden brown.

Place each hot pie on an individual serving plate and leave to stand for 5–10 minutes before serving, to cool slightly. Serve with a jug of warm crème anglaise or cream.

prune tartes fines

serves 6

These delectable puff tarts are so easy to make. Don't discard the leftover syrup – save it to serve with plain yoghurt for breakfast.

**750g ripe plums, ideally Victoria, or damsons
   or greengages, or a mixture, washed**
500ml stock syrup (page 275)
3 bay leaves
380g rough puff pastry (page 281)
200g crème patissière (page 273)
juice of ½ lemon

Cut the plums in half, remove the stones, then place in a dish. Put the stock syrup and bay leaves into a pan and bring to the boil, then leave to cool slightly for about 5 minutes. While still hot, pour the syrup over the plums, then set aside to cool.

On a lightly floured surface, roll out the pastry to a 2mm thickness. Using a 12cm cutter, cut out 6 rounds of pastry. Brush a baking sheet with a little cold water, then place the pastry rounds on the sheet. Chill for 20 minutes.

Preheat the oven to 180°C/Gas 4. Take the pastry rounds from the fridge and prick each one with a fork 5 or 6 times. Divide the crème patissière between the rounds, spreading it evenly, but leaving a 1cm margin around the edge. Carefully and thoroughly drain the plums, reserving the syrup. Arrange them on top of the crème patissière, skin side up or down as you prefer. Bake in the oven for 15–20 minutes, making sure the pastry is properly cooked on the bottom.

Use a palette knife to transfer the tarts to a wire rack and leave to cool slightly. Meanwhile, boil the reserved syrup in a pan to reduce to a semi-syrupy consistency, then add the lemon juice. Use a brush to coat the plums lightly with the reduced syrup. Place one tart on each plate and serve just slightly warm.

fig dartois

serves 6–8

> You can use raw figs and skip the syrup stage, if they are absolutely ripe and on the delicate side. The dartois can be made the day before and kept in the fridge until 2 or 3 hours before cooking.

1 litre stock syrup (page 275)
2 rosemary sprigs
10–14 ripe black or green figs (depending on size)
450g rough puff pastry (page 281)
150g frangipane (page 273)
1 egg yolk mixed with 1 tsp milk, to glaze
icing sugar, to dust

Bring the stock syrup to the boil in a pan with the rosemary added. Put the figs into a dish, pour on the boiling syrup and set aside to cool, then place the dish in the fridge.

On a lightly floured surface, roll out the puff pastry to a 28x24cm rectangle. Using a long-bladed knife, cut in half down the middle to make 2 strips, 28x12cm. Roll one strip around the rolling pin and unroll it onto a baking sheet, then place in the fridge.

Roll the other strip around the rolling pin, unroll onto a second baking sheet and prick lightly with a fork. Spread the frangipane over this pastry, leaving a 2cm margin around the edge. Drain the figs well, reserving the syrup, and arrange over the almond cream, leaving no gaps. Brush the pastry border with a little of the egg glaze.

Lightly flour the other pastry strip, then fold in half down its length without pressing the two sides together. Using a knife, make cuts at 3–4mm intervals down the folded side, stopping 2cm before the cut sides. Unfold the strip, roll it around the rolling pin and unfurl it on top of the fig-topped pastry. Using your fingertips, press the edges together to seal, then refrigerate for 30 minutes. Preheat the oven to 200°C/Gas 6.

Lightly brush the top of the dartois with glaze and trim the long edges, removing 2–3mm pastry. With the point of a knife, make little diagonal incisions along the edges. Bake for 25–30 minutes. Just before it is ready, take out the dartois, dust lightly

with icing sugar, then
return to the oven
for a final 2 minutes,
until nicely glazed.

As soon as you
remove it from the
oven, use a palette
knife to slide the
dartois onto a wire
rack to cool.

Serve the tart either
warm or at room
temperature, cut
into slices, with a
little of the poaching
syrup from the figs
on the side if you like.

tart tatin

serves 4–6

This is a favourite winter dessert at the Waterside Inn. We also sometimes make it using pears. Both versions are excellent with vanilla or cinnamon ice cream (pages 126 and 129).

5 medium apples, ideally Cox or Gala
juice of ½ lemon
120g butter, slightly softened
160g caster sugar
200g rough puff pastry (page 281)

Peel the apples and remove the cores using an apple corer, then cut each apple in half and sprinkle with the lemon juice. Cover the base of a 22–24cm diameter, 4–6cm deep ovenproof sauté pan, or a tarte tatin mould of similar dimensions, with the butter. Scatter the sugar evenly over the butter. Arrange the apple halves, rounded side down, on top, starting from the outside and working in towards the centre.

On a lightly floured surface, roll out the puff pastry to a round, 3mm thick and 2cm larger than the pan or mould. Prick the round with a fork in 6 or 8 places, roll it round a rolling pin and unfurl it over the apples. The pastry should extend beyond the edge of the apples by 1cm all around. Refrigerate for at least 20 minutes.

Preheat the oven to 180°C/Gas 4. Place the pan on the hob over a medium heat for 10 minutes. This is enough time for the butter and sugar to boil and take on a light amber colour. Using a small palette knife, lift the edge of the pastry all around the edge, to check that the underneath is beginning to caramelise evenly. Transfer to the oven and bake for 30 minutes, to cook the pastry and finish cooking the apples.

Leave to stand for 2–3 minutes, then briskly invert the tarte tatin onto a serving dish, using a dry tea towel to hold the dish and protect your hands. If the apples have shifted a little while being inverted, move them gently back into place with the tip of a knife. Serve immediately.

A simple dessert that can be assembled at short notice, as long as
you have beautifully ripe, sweet berries to hand. The mint and pepper
play an important role in accentuating the flavours of the fruit.

100g caster sugar
200g small blackberries (or halved if large)
200g small strawberries
200g raspberries
10g mint leaves, snipped at the last minute
black pepper (in a mill)
150g butter, melted, plus extra to grease
10 sheets of ready-made filo or brick pastry

Melt the sugar in a large, non-stick saucepan over a medium heat. As soon as it starts
to caramelise lightly, add the blackberries. A minute later add the strawberries, and
2 minutes after that add the raspberries. Cook for 3 minutes. Now add the mint, give
4 or 5 turns of the pepper mill, then drain the fruits in a sieve set over a bowl to catch
the juice. Tip the juice into a small saucepan and let bubble over a gentle heat until
reduced to a semi-syrupy consistency, then set aside with the drained fruits to cool.

Preheat the oven to 180°C/Gas 4. Butter an 18–20cm cake tin with removable base.
Brush 3 sheets of filo with melted butter and layer lightly in the tin, letting the excess
filo overhang the sides of the tin. Scatter a third of the drained fruit on top, then butter
another 2 sheets of filo and layer on top of the fruit. Scatter half of the remaining fruit
over this pastry layer, then cover with another 2 buttered sheets of filo. Scatter the
remaining fruit over this layer and cover with the last 3 sheets of filo, buttering them
first. Fold the overhanging edges of filo back towards the middle.

Cook in the oven for 15–20 minutes, until the pastry is very pale nutty brown in colour.
Leave to stand for 5–10 minutes before serving.

To unmould, carefully push up the removable base and slide the red berry filo gently
off the base and onto a serving dish. Pour the reduced juices decoratively over the top
and serve at once.

serves 6

This recent creation of my son Alain is proving to be very popular at the Waterside Inn. It's an airy mille-feuille, light as a feather and filled with a delectable vanilla cream and strawberries. The icing sugar glaze has a lovely sheen.

240g rough puff pastry (page 281)
60g icing sugar
1 sheet leaf gelatine
350ml warm crème anglaise (at 80°C),
    well flavoured with vanilla (page 56)
50ml whipping cream
300g strawberries, cut into 2–3mm slices

Roll out the pastry on a lightly floured surface to a 36x12cm rectangle, 4mm thick. Cut into six 12x6cm pieces and lift onto a baking sheet. Refrigerate for 20 minutes.

Preheat the oven to 180°C/Gas 4. Stand a 3cm high ring or mould in each corner of the baking sheet and put another baking sheet on top, resting on the moulds so that the pastry will be lightly compressed as it cooks. Bake for 15 minutes, then lower the setting to 170°C/Gas 3 and cook for a further 10 minutes. Take out of the oven and remove the top baking sheet and rings. Raise the oven temperature to 230°C/Gas 8. Dust the mille-feuilles with the icing sugar and return to the oven for 2–3 minutes to glaze; don't let them burn. Using a palette knife, transfer to a wire rack to cool.

Soak the gelatine in cold water for 5 minutes, then drain, squeeze out excess water and add to the warm custard, stirring until melted. Let cool, then chill for 4–5 hours to set. Whisk to loosen. Whip the cream to soft peaks, then fold into the custard. Put into a piping bag fitted with a Saint Honoré or 1.5cm fluted nozzle and chill for 30 minutes.

Using a serrated knife, trim the pastry edges to neaten, then cut each one horizontally into three, to make 3 layers for each mille-feuille. Arrange the strawberry slices on the bottom layers, cover with the middle layers and pipe the crème anglaise generously over this layer. Finally, place the glazed pastry layer on top and press it lightly down to bond the layers. Use a palette knife to slide the mille-feuilles onto plates and serve.

mini croquembouche

serves 6–8 illustrated on previous page

choux pastry
125ml milk
100g butter, diced, plus extra to grease
½ tsp salt
1 tsp caster sugar
150g plain flour
4 eggs
1 egg yolk mixed with 2 tsp milk, to glaze

to assemble
250g caster sugar
40g liquid glucose
150ml double cream
250g crème patissière (page 273)
1 tbsp Grand Marnier
2 tsp groundnut oil, to oil the mould

to decorate (optional)
20 candied violet petals
150g mimosa balls

Preheat the oven to 180°C/Gas 4. To make the choux pastry, combine the milk, 125ml water, the butter, salt and sugar in a saucepan and set over a low heat. Bring to the boil and immediately take the pan off the heat. Shower in the flour and mix with a wooden spoon until smooth. Return the pan to a medium heat and stir for about 1 minute to dry out the paste, then tip it into a bowl. Add the eggs one at a time, beating with the wooden spoon. Once the eggs are all incorporated, the paste should be smooth and shiny with a thick ribbon consistency. It's now ready to use.

Put the choux pastry into a piping bag fitted with a 5–7cm plain nozzle. Pipe into balls about 1cm in diameter onto a buttered baking sheet; you will need 48 in total. Brush with the egg glaze and bake for 10 minutes, until dry and crisp, but still soft inside. If necessary, switch off the oven off and leave the choux balls inside for a few minutes, to dry them out. Transfer them to a wire rack. Once they have cooled completely, make a little hole with a knife in the base of each choux ball.

To make the caramel, dissolve the sugar in 80ml water in a small saucepan over a medium heat, then bring to the boil and skim. Add the liquid glucose and heat until it reaches 160°C, using a brush dipped in cold water to brush down any crystals forming on the inside of the pan. Immediately remove from the heat. Partially dip each choux ball into the caramel to coat the top third and then place on a tray. Leave until set.

A majestic dessert for special occasions. Your guests will marvel at your amazing talent… a bit of courage is all you need to pull it off.

In a bowl, whip the cream to a ribbon consistency, then fold into the crème patissière with the Grand Marnier. Put the mixture into a piping bag fitted with a 3–5mm plain nozzle and use to fill the choux balls, piping it in through the hole in the base.

Warm the remaining caramel over a very gentle heat. Oil the inside of a rigid metal cone or chinois, about 18cm in diameter and 18cm tall. Place a choux ball in the base of the cone, with the caramel side facing into the pointed end. Gently spear another choux ball with the tip of a small knife and dip one-fifth of one side into the warm caramel (just enough to pick up a dab), then stick it onto one side of the first choux ball, so that the cooled caramel side is against the inside of the cone. The warm caramel will stick this choux ball to the first choux ball. Proceed in this way with the remaining choux balls, arranging them up the sides of the cone and keeping the top level regular and straight as it grows, until you have used all the choux balls. The croquembouche is now fully assembled.

Wait a few minutes for the caramel to cool completely, then give the croquembouche a gentle turn to make sure it's not stuck to the mould. Invert the cone onto a serving dish and remove to release the croquembouche. Dip the tips of the violet petals, if using, into the caramel and, working quickly, stick them at intervals between the choux balls. Arrange the mimosa balls, if using, around the base and serve.

kataifi

Excellent chef pâtissier, Andonis, taught me how to make these sweet, spicy, nutty Greek pastries. They will keep in an airtight container for 3–4 days. Kataifi dough is available from Greek food stores.

200g butter, melted (ideally clarified, page 283)
500g ready-made kataifi dough

syrup
600g caster sugar
100g liquid glucose
1 cinnamon stick, broken into pieces
juice of 1 lemon

filling
125g walnuts, roughly chopped
125g shelled unsalted pistachio nuts,
  roughly chopped
1 tsp ground cinnamon
50g sugared biscuits, crumbled
generous pinch of ground cloves

For the syrup, pour 400ml water into a saucepan, add the sugar, liquid glucose, cinnamon and lemon juice and dissolve the sugar over a medium heat. Bring to the boil, then lower the heat and simmer for 10 minutes. Leave to cool until warm, then strain the syrup through a chinois or sieve into a bowl.

Generously brush a 22cm round cake tin, 4cm deep, with some of the butter. To make the filling, put all the ingredients into a bowl and add enough of the warm syrup (about 50ml) to bring the mixture together – it should be firm and compact.

On a clean surface, ease apart the kataifi strands to loosen any that are densely packed and to create a little space between them. Take about 35g of the dough and form it into an upside-down T shape, 10cm tall and 8cm across the bar, with the bar nearest to you. Place about 20g of the filling in the middle of the bar, bring the sides of the bar over it and firmly roll up to the end of the T, without crushing the dough strands, so that the kataifi dough envelops the filling. Place in the prepared cake tin.

Repeat with the remaining dough and filling to make about 15 kataifi in total, placing them in the tin so they fit snugly, but are not too tightly packed. Brush them very generously with the remaining butter. Use the back of a small knife to delineate one kataifi from another. Leave to stand for 1 hour. Preheat the oven to 180°C/Gas 4.

Bake the kataifi for 30 minutes. In the meantime, warm the remaining syrup. As you take the kataifi from the oven, spoon three-quarters of the syrup over them. Leave for 30 minutes, then drizzle the rest of the syrup over.

Cover with a clean tea towel and leave to stand for 4–5 hours, before removing from the tin and separating out each kataifi. Serve with coffee.

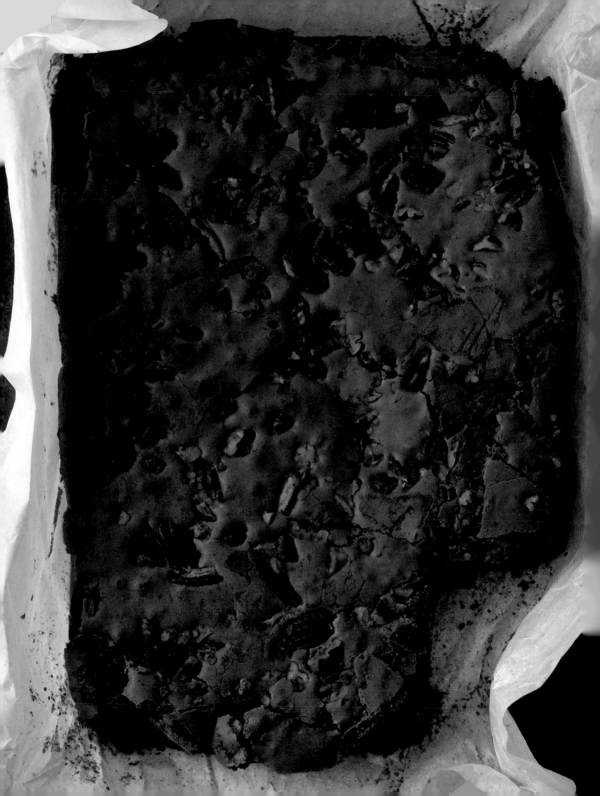

These recipes, with the exception of the final mousse cake, are all easygoing and adaptable. Suitable to round off any meal – brunch, lunch, teatime, picnic or dinner – they will fit in anywhere. The chocolate mousse cake with cherries is velvety smooth and delicate, and it really does need to be served chilled. Do try both the cheesecakes: they are silky and rich, but surprisingly light. And I strongly recommend my recipe for pain d'épices. Here's a little culinary tip from my childhood: smear salted butter over a slice of it, cover with coarsely grated dark, bitter chocolate, then sink your teeth in!

cakes & gâteaux

lemon cake

makes 2, each serving 6

50g butter, melted and cooled, plus extra to grease
3 small eggs, at room temperature
175g caster sugar
finely grated zest of 2 lemons
pinch of salt
75ml double cream
140g plain flour

1 tsp baking powder
50ml dark rum
80g apricot jam, sieved

icing
80g icing sugar
juice of 1 lemon

Preheat the oven to 190°C/Gas 5. Grease 2 loaf tins, 12.5x5cm base measurement, about 5cm deep, with butter and line with greaseproof paper.

Lightly whisk the eggs, sugar, lemon zest and salt together in a bowl with a balloon whisk for 20 seconds. Still whisking, pour in the cream and whisk just until combined.

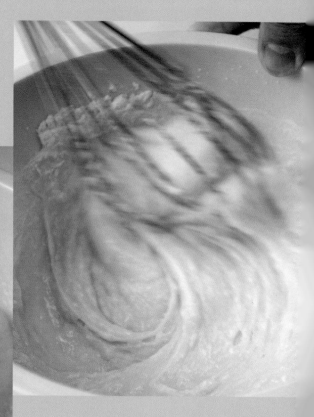

Sift in the flour with the baking powder and whisk to mix for 30 seconds. Add all but 2 tsp of the rum, stirring with the whisk until just incorporated.

The delicate, dainty nature of this cake makes it an ideal dessert – just as it is, or with seasonal fruits – or a lovely treat with tea or coffee at any time of the day. It will keep in an airtight container in a cool place for 3–4 days, or you can freeze it.

Now pour in the cooled, melted butter and mix until evenly combined, without overworking.

Divide the mixture between the prepared tins and bake for 5 minutes, then lower the oven setting to 180°C/Gas 4 and cook for a further 25 minutes, until golden.

continued overleaf

Immediately unmould the cakes onto a wire rack. Sprinkle the remaining rum over the surface, remove the greaseproof paper and leave to cool. Turn the oven up to 240°C/Gas 9.

Heat the apricot jam in a small pan until just bubbling, then take off the heat. Brush the tops and sides of the cakes generously with the jam, then leave on the wire rack for 5 minutes.

Mix the icing sugar and lemon juice in a bowl to form a smooth icing, then spoon over the tops of the cakes, still on the rack and with a baking tray placed underneath to catch any excess. Place the cakes in the oven for 20 seconds, just enough time for the lemon icing to set as a glaze. Leave to cool completely. Serve cut into thin slices.

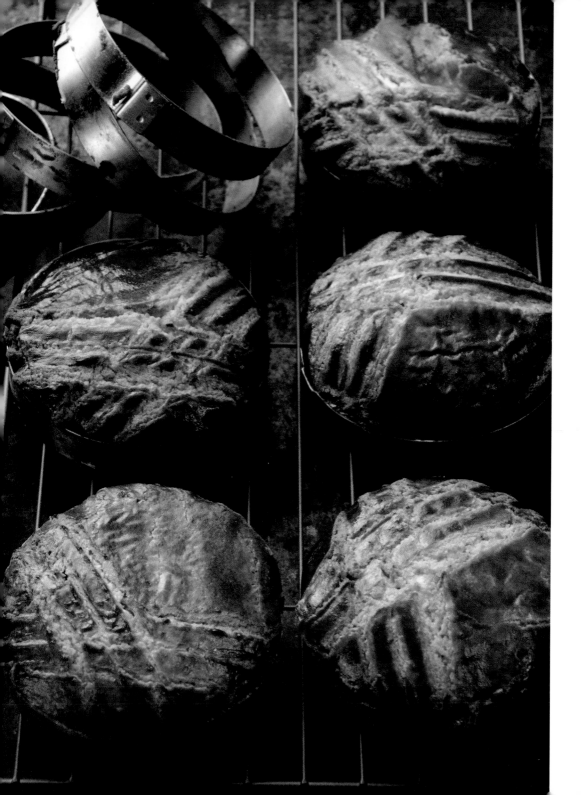

serves 6

These individual cakes are delicious served with a rhubarb compote or vanilla ice cream (page 126), or with homemade jam.

180g salted butter, softened, plus extra to grease
4 egg yolks
140g caster sugar
pinch of salt
2 tsp runny honey
1 tbsp dark rum
225g plain flour
1 egg yolk mixed with 2 tsp milk, to glaze

Preheat the oven to 170°C/Gas 3. Lightly butter 6 metal rings, 8cm in diameter and 1.5cm tall, and place on a baking sheet lined with baking parchment.

Whisk the egg yolks, sugar and salt together in a large bowl to a ribbon consistency.

In another bowl, whisk the butter until lightly creamed, then incorporate the honey and rum. Add to the egg yolk mixture and mix until evenly combined. Finally, whisk in the flour, a little at a time.

Spoon the mixture into the metal rings, dividing it evenly, and spread it level with a palette knife. Lightly brush the surface of each cake with the glaze, then use the back of a fork to lightly mark a criss-cross pattern across the top (as shown). Bake for 18 minutes.

As soon as you take the cakes out of the oven, remove the metal rings and transfer the cakes to a wire rack to cool slightly. Serve warm.

You can bake one large cake instead if you like, in an 18–20cm loose-based cake tin, increasing the cooking time to 35 minutes.

glacé fruit cake

makes 10–12 slices

This lovely cake freezes well, but the glaze and topping are best
applied after thawing – for 12 hours in the fridge, then a further 12 hours
at room temperature.

100g raisins
50ml dark rum, plus an extra 50ml to
    sprinkle
125g butter, softened, plus extra to grease
125g icing sugar, sifted
2 eggs, at room temperature, plus 1 egg yolk
1 large vanilla pod, split lengthways

190g plain flour
1 tsp baking powder
100g glacé cherries, preferably Bigarreau
100g other mixed glacé fruits
75g apricot glaze or sieved apricot jam,
    warmed
50g mixed glacé fruits, to decorate

Soak the raisins in the rum for 15 minutes. Whisk the butter and icing sugar together in
a large bowl for 1 minute. Beat in the whole eggs one at a time, followed by the egg yolk.
Scrape the vanilla seeds into the mixture and mix until evenly combined. Sift about
four-fifths of the flour with the baking powder over the mixture and fold in carefully.

Toss the raisins, glacé cherries and other glacé fruits with the remaining flour. Fold
into the cake mixture, without overworking. Cover and refrigerate for 10 minutes.

Preheat the oven to 200°C/Gas 6. Butter a loaf tin, about 20x8cm and 7cm deep,
and line with greaseproof paper, making sure it extends 2–3cm above the rim. Spoon
the cake mixture into the tin and spread evenly. Bake for 5 minutes, then lower the
setting to 180°C/Gas 4 and cook for a further 30–40 minutes, or until a skewer inserted
into the centre comes out clean.

As you take the cake from the oven, sprinkle the rum over the surface. Leave in the tin
for 10–15 minutes then remove and transfer to a wire rack to cool. Using scissors, snip
the excess greaseproof paper decoratively (as shown). Lightly brush the surface of the
cake with the warmed apricot glaze, then arrange glacé fruits over the top to decorate.
The cake is best served at least 12 hours after being cooked, cut into thin slices.

illustrated on previous page

This lovely 'bread of spices' – similar to gingerbread – is delicious topped with poached pear or peach slices as a dessert. Poach the fruit in stock syrup (page 275), with star anise and cloves and let it cool before slicing.

35g butter, cut into small pieces, plus extra to grease
310g plain flour, plus extra to dust
625g runny honey
1 large egg
60ml milk
½ tsp ground cinnamon
½ tsp ground ginger

¼ tsp freshly grated nutmeg
¼ tsp ground cloves
pinch of ground cardamom
2 tsp bicarbonate of soda
½ tsp fine salt
50g candied orange peel (see page 258, or shop-bought), cut into very small dice

Preheat the oven to 160°C/Gas 3. Butter and flour a terrine mould (ideally cast iron), about 30x10cm and 8cm deep.

Warm the honey and butter in a heatproof bowl set over a saucepan of hot water on a medium heat until the mixture reaches 30°C. Remove the bowl from the heat, then whisk in the egg and milk without overworking. Sift the flour, spices, bicarbonate of soda and salt over the mixture and fold in, using a rubber spatula, until evenly combined. Now fold in the candied orange peel.

Tip the mixture into the prepared mould and immediately place in the oven. Bake for 1 hour–1 hour 10 minutes, or until a fine skewer inserted into the centre comes out clean. Leave in the tin for a minute or so before turning out onto a wire rack. Leave to cool completely.

This loaf cake is ready to serve a few hours after being cooked, or it can be wrapped in cling film and kept in the fridge for up to 2 weeks. To serve, cut into slices and offer it to your guests, with butter (ideally salted) on the side if you like.

NOTE In France you can buy pain d'épices spice mix, which is a blend of the spices I have used above, though the composition does vary. If you happen to have some, use 6g pain d'épices spice mix.

pecan nut brownies

Everyone adores brownies. They are easy to make and keep for several days in an airtight container in a cool place. I like to serve them with crème anglaise (page 56) or a spoonful of crème fraîche.

200g butter, cut into small pieces,
    plus extra to grease
200g good-quality dark chocolate, 70% cocoa
    solids (preferably Valrhona), cut into small pieces
4 eggs
220g light brown sugar
120g plain flour
220g pecan nuts, cut into large pieces

Butter a 24x34cm baking tin, 6cm deep, and line with greaseproof paper, allowing the paper to extend above the rim of the tin (to assist unmoulding). Preheat the oven to 190°C/Gas 5.

Melt the butter and chocolate in a heatproof bowl set over a pan of barely simmering water. Stir until smooth, then remove the bowl from the pan and set aside to cool slightly.

Using an electric mixer, beat the eggs for 2 minutes, then add the brown sugar and beat until the mixture reaches a ribbon consistency, about 6 minutes. Using a spatula, incorporate into the melted chocolate, but do not overwork. Add the flour and nuts in a steady stream, folding them in with the spatula just until evenly mixed; stop mixing at this point.

Pour the mixture into the prepared tin and immediately place in the oven. Cook for 20–25 minutes, lowering the oven setting to 180°C/Gas 4 after 10 minutes. To test, insert a skewer or knife tip into the centre; it should come out clean and shiny. Set aside to cool in the tin.

Once cooled, lift out the brownie, using the lining paper. Cut into squares or smaller pieces and serve in an artful heap.

illustrated on previous page

serves 6–8

Bitter almonds give this light base-less cheesecake a lovely fragrance. This prized recipe, called *ostkaka*, comes from Småland in Sweden and was introduced to me by my Swedish friends, the Magnusson family.

3.3 litres milk
120g plain flour
2 tsp liquid rennet
butter, to grease
2 eggs

110g caster sugar
6 bitter almonds, grated (on a medium grater)
200ml double cream
20g icing sugar, to dust
240g strawberries or raspberries, to serve

Heat 3 litres of the milk in a large saucepan until it reaches 37°C. Meanwhile, pour the remaining 300ml milk into a bowl and mix in the flour and rennet with a whisk. When the milk is at 37°C, add the flour and rennet mixture, then transfer to a bowl. Leave to stand for 40 minutes, until semi-set.

Using a knife, make several deep incisions in the semi-set milk and stir very lightly with a wooden spoon. Line a large sieve (that will take the milk) with a layer of muslin, leaving plenty overhanging, and set it over a deep bowl. Carefully pour in the semi-set milk. After 5 minutes, bring the muslin up over the milk and place in the fridge. Leave to drain for 1 hour. About 1.9 litres liquid will drain out in this time.

Preheat the oven to 170°C/Gas 3. Butter a shallow ovenproof dish, about 26x20cm. Whisk the eggs and sugar together in a bowl until thickened almost to a ribbon consistency, then incorporate the grated almonds. Tip the drained milk from the sieve into a large bowl and fold in the whisked mixture, followed by the double cream.

Pour the mixture into the prepared dish and bake for 55 minutes, then check to see if it is cooked by inserting a skewer into the middle; if it comes out clean, the cheesecake is cooked. Leave to cool completely.

Dust the cheesecake with icing sugar and serve with the strawberries or raspberries.

new york cheesecake

serves 8–10

A cheesecake known the world over, though there are endless variations on the recipe. Having tasted so many, I am delighted to be able to offer you this stunningly good version!

base
65g butter, melted, plus 20g to grease
250g digestive biscuits

filling
1kg cream cheese, softened
2 tbsp milk
350g caster sugar
35g plain flour
very finely grated zest of 1 orange
very finely grated zest of 1 lemon
5 eggs, plus 2 egg yolks
1 vanilla pod, split lengthways

Preheat the oven to 180°C/Gas 4. Lightly butter a 22–24cm springform cake tin, 5–6cm deep, and place on a baking sheet. Crush the biscuits in a food processor to crumbs, transfer to a bowl, add the melted butter and mix until thoroughly combined. Tip the biscuit mixture into the cake tin and spread to form a uniform layer, pressing it firmly and evenly. Bake for 12 minutes, until firm. Set aside to cool, still on the baking sheet.

Raise the oven setting to 220°C/Gas 7. Using an electric mixer, beat the cream cheese, milk, sugar, flour and citrus zests together until evenly combined, smooth and lightly creamy. On a low speed, incorporate the eggs one at a time, followed by the egg yolks. Finally, add the vanilla seeds from the pod. Scrape down the sides of the bowl a few times during mixing, to ensure the filling is homogeneous.

Pour the filling over the biscuit base in the tin and bake for 12 minutes, then lower the oven setting to 100°C/Gas ¼ and cook for a further 1 hour. Turn the oven off and leave the cheesecake inside with the door slightly ajar for 1 hour to cool slowly; this helps to prevent the surface from cracking. Transfer the cheesecake in its tin to a wire rack to cool completely, then refrigerate for at least 6 hours before serving.

To serve, carefully unmould the cheesecake and cut into slices, using a very sharp knife dipped in hot water between each cut.

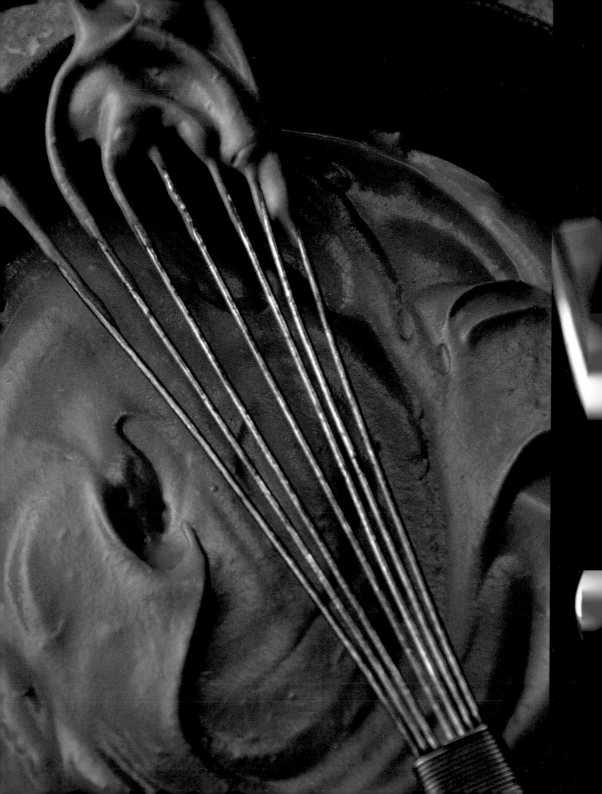

chocolate mousse cake with cherries

serves 8–10

20cm chocolate Genoese sponge (page 163)

cherry compote
400g perfectly ripe black cherries, stoned
150g caster sugar
finely pared zest of 1 orange
2 cloves

chocolate mousse
200g good-quality dark chocolate, 70% cocoa
  solids (preferably Valrhona), in pieces
200ml hot crème anglaise (page 56)
200ml double cream

to serve
chocolate shavings (see below)

For the cherry compote, put the cherries into a saucepan, add enough cold water to just cover and the sugar, orange zest and cloves. Cook over a gentle heat for 20–30 minutes, depending on the size and ripeness of the cherries, until soft. Remove from the heat and leave the cherries to cool in their poaching syrup.

To make the chocolate mousse, put the chocolate into a bowl and pour on the hot crème anglaise (it should be between 75 and 85°C), stirring with a wooden spoon. Now use a balloon whisk to mix until smooth; the mixture should now be just warm. Whip the cream in another bowl to a ribbon consistency and fold into the mixture until evenly combined; do not overwork.

Drain the cherries well, reserving the poaching syrup; discard the cloves and orange zest. Pour one-third of the syrup into a small pan, bring to the boil and let bubble until reduced to a syrupy consistency, then mix with one-third of the cherries. Reserve this cherry compote for serving.

Carefully split the chocolate sponge horizontally, into two even layers. Using a brush, daub the cut surfaces with the remaining cherry poaching syrup. To assemble, place a 22cm flan ring on a flat plate. Lay the top half of the sponge, cut side up, inside the ring. Using a spoon and a small palette knife, spread a layer of chocolate mousse over

illustrated on previous page

This sensational dessert is well worth the effort. It can be made a day or two in advance, and the fresh cherries can be replaced with good-quality tinned or jarred ones.

the sponge to a thickness of 1.5cm. Fill the gap between the ring and the sponge with mousse. Sprinkle the remaining drained cherries over the mousse and press them in lightly. Place the second sponge, cut side down, on top. Using your fingertips, lightly press down, then spread a thin layer of mousse on top. Smooth with a palette knife and refrigerate for at least 4 hours, until ready to serve.

To serve, briefly heat the outside of the flan ring using a cook's blowtorch or a hot tea towel, then lift off the ring, using small rotating movements. Gently press some chocolate shavings around the sides, then generously cover the top of the cake with the rest of the shavings.

Using a very sharp fine-bladed knife dipped into hot water, cut the mousse cake into slices. Place a slice on each place, with a spoonful of cherry compote alongside. Serve very cold, with cream if you like.

chocolate shavings Using a vegetable peeler, shave curls from a block of good-quality dark chocolate. For more impressive curls, melt dark couverture chocolate, spread evenly on a marble slab and allow to almost set, then shave off curls with a long-bladed knife, or scraper held at a 45° angle.

Variously shaped, these diminutive, enticing and elegant delicacies are usually offered at the end of a meal, with coffee. With the exception of the tuiles, which are considerably larger, they are best eaten in a single mouthful. Most petits fours can be stored in airtight containers for several days, so their pleasure extends beyond a single occasion. Chocolates are, of course, always popular, not least the decadent truffles overleaf, but I love all the treats in this chapter. I recommend that you serve just one or two petits fours as the finale to a meal, rather than an assortment, to fully appreciate their qualities.

chocolates &
petits fours

chocolate truffles

makes 80

These quantities can be halved, but since truffles freeze well and make perfect gifts, I suggest you prepare the full quantity.

**750g good-quality dark chocolate, 70% cocoa
   solids (preferably Valrhona), roughly chopped
150ml double cream
225g butter, in pieces, at room temperature
35ml Armagnac, brandy or Grand Marnier
about 500g good-quality cocoa powder**

Add the butter a little at a time, still whisking and without overworking. Now pour in the Armagnac or other alcohol, stirring gently with a whisk until mixed. Set aside to cool for about an hour, to allow the chocolate 'ganache' to firm up a little.

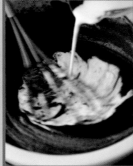

Put 450g of the chocolate into a heatproof bowl and set over a saucepan one-third filled with hot water, making sure that the bottom of the bowl is not touching the water. Place over a gentle heat (the water should not exceed 50–60°C). As soon as the chocolate has melted, remove the bowl from the heat.

Bring the cream to the boil in a small pan. As soon as it boils, remove from the heat and set aside until cooled to about 40°C. Add the cream to the chocolate, mixing it in with a balloon whisk until smooth.

Put the mixture into a piping bag fitted with a 1–1.5cm plain nozzle and pipe small mounds, about 2cm in diameter, onto trays lined with greaseproof paper. Refrigerate for 2 hours.

Roll each piped mound in the palm of your hand for 3–5 seconds, to make little balls. Chill until you are ready to dip and coat the truffles.

Melt the remaining 300g chocolate (as before). Spread the cocoa powder on a work surface or tray. Using a small fork or round dipping tool, dip the truffles, one at a time, into the melted chocolate for 1–2 seconds to coat, then immediately place in the cocoa powder and turn with a fork to roll and coat in the cocoa.

Transfer the coated truffles to a fine-meshed wire rack and set aside in a cool but not humid place until ready to serve or pack into freezerproof containers. Best served with coffee.

chocolate and almond rochers

makes 36–40

You can make these using white chocolate couverture if you prefer. As you are shaping the rochers, work swiftly as the mixture has a tendency to solidify; if it does, just warm the mixture over hot water for a minute to soften.

250g nibbed almonds
50ml Cognac or Armagnac
50g icing sugar, sifted
200g dark bitter chocolate, 60–70% cocoa solids
   (preferably Valrhona), chopped
30ml cocoa butter or hazelnut oil, gently warmed

Preheat the oven to 180°C/Gas 4. In a bowl, toss the almonds with the Cognac or Armagnac. Dust with the icing sugar and mix to ensure the almond pieces are evenly coated. Scatter on a baking sheet lined with baking parchment and toast in the oven for 10–12 minutes, turning them at least twice, until evenly golden. Set aside to cool, moving them about with a palette knife every 5 minutes so they don't stick together.

Put the chocolate into a heatproof bowl and place over a pan one-third filled with hot water (at 50–60°C), making sure the bowl does not touch the water. Melt over a gentle heat, making sure the temperature of the chocolate doesn't exceed 50°C.

In another bowl, mix about one-third of the almonds with one-third of the warmed cocoa butter or hazelnut oil until the almonds are nicely glossy. Pour one-third of the melted chocolate over the almonds and mix gently until evenly coated.

Drop a dessertspoonful of the mixture onto a sheet of baking parchment, to form a little mound. Shape the rest of the mixture in this way, working quickly and leaving 2–3cm between each rocher. Repeat to mix and shape the rest of the rochers, in 2 batches. Leave in a cool but not humid place, until set, about 15–20 minutes.

Store in airtight containers, interleaved with greaseproof paper, in the fridge until ready to use. To serve, place the rochers in petits fours cases on a platter.

candied grapefruit or orange peel

These are lovely as they are, or coated in chocolate – simply dip in melted chocolate one by one using a small fork. I also use the strips of peel diced in desserts and cakes (see pages 65 and 241).

3 grapefruit or 6 oranges
600g caster sugar
75g granulated sugar, to coat

Using a sharp, flexible knife, cut a 5mm slice from the base of each fruit. Starting at the top and following the contour of the fruit towards the base, cut 7 strips of peel, including the white pith, 3cm wide, from each grapefruit, or 5 strips from each orange. Cut each strip into baton shapes, 1cm wide.

Put these strips of citrus peel into a saucepan, cover with cold water and bring to the boil. Drain and refresh in cold water, then drain again. Repeat this procedure 4 times.

Dissolve the caster sugar in 450ml water in another saucepan over a low heat. Bring slowly to the boil and skim the surface if necessary. Immerse the blanched strips of peel in the syrup and poach at a bare simmer for 2 hours for the orange, or 3 hours for grapefruit.

Leave the strips to cool in the syrup until warm, then drain and place on a wire rack to finishing cooling, keeping them apart. Finally, roll in the granulated sugar to coat.

Store in an airtight container in the fridge until ready to serve, interleaved with parchment or cellophane to stop them sticking together. They will keep for a week.

Serve the candied peel strips on their own or alongside blackcurrant pâte de fruits (right), with a glass of Cognac, or just a coffee.

makes 25–30 pieces

These intensely flavoured little squares of chewy fruit jelly keep well for a week stored in a cool, dry place.

200g fresh unsweetened blackcurrant purée,
    or ready-made frozen (Boiron is a good
    brand) and defrosted
210g caster sugar
15g yellow pectin
1–2 tsp lemon juice
60g granulated sugar, to coat

Put the blackcurrant purée into a heavy-based saucepan and boil over a medium heat for 2 minutes. Mix 90g of the caster sugar with the pectin and add to the purée. Boil for a further minute. Now add the remaining 120g caster sugar and cook until the mixture registers 103°C on a cook's thermometer. Remove from the heat, add the lemon juice and stir with a whisk. Set aside to rest for 20 seconds.

Place a sheet of greaseproof paper on a marble surface or baking sheet. Place a 15cm square metal confectionery frame, or caramel rulers set to make a 15cm square, on the greaseproof paper. Pour the very hot mixture into the frame or between the rulers and leave to cool for about 3 hours.

When cool, remove the frame or rulers and cut the pâte de fruits block into 2.5–3cm squares, using a sharp, long-bladed knife (or a confectionery 'guitar' cutter if you have one). Dip the top and bottom surfaces of the squares in the granulated sugar to coat, leaving the sides uncoated.

Serve the pâte de fruits on their own or with candied citrus peel strips (left).

Depending on the season, you can make pâté de fruits with apricots or strawberries, provided the fruit is perfectly ripe and full of flavour.

makes 26–30

½ egg white
150g good-quality almond paste (ideally
    50% sugar)
15 blanched almonds
1 stick preserved angelica, cut into 15 small
    diamonds, or 7–8 glacé cherries, halved

Line a large baking tray with baking parchment. On a clean work surface or in a
bowl, work the egg white into the almond paste, at first using your fingertips, then
pummelling a few times with the palm of your hand. Put the almond paste into
a piping bag fitted with a 1cm fluted nozzle and pipe into teardrop or comma shapes
on the prepared tray.

Place a whole almond on top of half of them, and an angelica diamond or halved
glacé cherry on the rest, pressing them in lightly so they adhere. Set aside in a warm
spot (25–30°C) for about 8 hours, until a slight crust has formed on the surface.

Preheat the oven to 180°C/Gas 4. Bake the petits fours for 6–7 minutes. On removing
from the oven, trickle a little cold water between the parchment and baking tray.
After 2–3 minutes, lift off the petits fours and place on a wire rack to cool.

Serve on their own or with a selection of other petits fours, with tea or coffee.

Brushing a glaze of stock syrup (page 275) over these petits fours
as you take them from the oven will give them a beautiful shine. They keep
well in an airtight tin for 3 days.

madeleines with honey and pink pepper

makes 36–40

2 large eggs
70g caster sugar
15g soft brown sugar
pinch of salt
90g plain flour
½ tsp baking powder
90g butter, melted and slightly cooled, plus
   30g melted, to grease
10g runny honey
½ tsp freeze-dried pink peppercorns, crushed

Lightly beat the eggs, both sugars and the salt together in a bowl with a wooden spoon, until the mixture begins to turn pale. Sift the flour with the baking powder over the mixture and beat for 30 seconds to incorporate.

Pour in the 90g melted butter and the honey, mix together until smooth, then add the crushed pink pepper. Cover and set aside in a cool place (but not the fridge) for 20 minutes. Preheat the oven to 220°C/Gas 7.

Grease 2 mini madeleine trays (or other small moulds) with melted butter. Put the mixture into a large piping bag fitted with a 1cm plain nozzle and pipe little, even domes into the moulds, shaping about 36–40 in total.

Bake the madeleines for 4–5 minutes, taking care not to cook them for any longer or they will lose their soft texture. As soon as they are cooked, turn them out straight onto a wire rack, making sure you don't crush any of them as you do so. They are at their best served just warm.

These adorable mini madeleines are irresistible. They keep well for 4–5 days in an airtight container but are at their best eaten warm from the oven. You can also serve them with floating islands (page 161) or raspberry mousse (page 172).

chocolate-dipped langues de chat

makes 40

A lovely, classic petits four to serve with coffee, these also go very well with many fruit desserts, as well as with ice cream.

125g butter, softened
125g icing sugar
25g ground almonds
3 egg whites
165g plain flour
1 vanilla pod, split lengthways and seeds
   scraped out (optional)
200g good-quality dark chocolate, 70% cocoa
   solids (preferably Valrhona), cut into pieces

Beat the butter and 100g of the icing sugar together in a bowl with a wooden spoon for 1 minute. Sift the ground almonds and remaining 25g icing sugar together over the mixture, then stir in. Incorporate the egg whites one at a time, then finally mix in the flour and vanilla seeds, if using. Cover the bowl with cling film and set aside for at least 20 minutes to rest.

Preheat the oven to 190°C/Gas 5. Transfer the mixture to a piping bag fitted with a 1cm plain nozzle. Pipe 6–7cm neat lengths onto a non-stick baking sheet (or regular sheet lightly buttered and dusted with flour), leaving about 2cm between each one.

Bake for 5–6 minutes, until lightly coloured. Use a small palette knife to transfer the langues de chat to a wire rack and leave to cool.

Gently melt the chocolate in a heatproof bowl set over a pan of barely simmering water. One at a time, partially dip the langues de chat into the melted chocolate to half-coat them, then place flat side down on a tray lined with baking parchment and leave until the chocolate has set.

Store interleaved with greaseproof paper in an airtight container in a cool, dry place until ready to serve.

illustrated on previous page

These are the most prized petits fours at the Waterside Inn. They keep well in an airtight container in the fridge for several days, but are even more delicious when they have just emerged, still warm, from the oven...

40g plain flour
¼ tsp baking powder
120g icing sugar, sifted, plus extra to dust
45g ground almonds
pinch of vanilla sugar, or a very small pinch of
   pure ground vanilla
4 egg whites, at room temperature
65g butter
52 small, ripe raspberries, or 26 large ones, halved

Sift the flour and baking powder into a bowl, add the icing sugar, ground almonds and vanilla and stir to mix. Add the egg whites and mix well with a wooden spoon for 1 minute.

Heat the butter in a small pan over a medium heat, until it reaches 45–50°C, i.e. the beurre noisette stage. Immediately tip the butter into the financier mixture and mix well to combine. Leave to rest for 5–10 minutes. Preheat the oven to 170°C/Gas 3.

Transfer the mixture to a piping bag fitted with a 1cm plain nozzle. Pipe into a non-stick silicone mould with rectangular-shaped indentations, 5cm long, 3cm wide and 2cm deep (or lightly buttered metal moulds with indentations of similar dimensions), three-quarters filling them. Place 2 raspberries or raspberry halves in each, and bake for 10–12 minutes.

Leave the financiers in the moulds for 1–2 minutes before carefully transferring to a wire rack to cool.

Dust the financiers lightly with icing sugar before serving with coffee or tea.

illustrated on page 264

makes 20–24

You can make these any size you like, from 6–10cm in diameter. They are delicate, fragile, crisp and delicious. They keep well in sealed containers for 4–5 days, but are best eaten soon after baking.

2 whole eggs, plus 1 egg white
125g caster sugar
20ml double cream
37.5g plain flour
½ vanilla pod, split lengthways
125g flaked almonds
40g butter, to grease
25g icing sugar, to dust

Lightly beat the eggs and egg white in a bowl with a fork for 10 seconds. Add the sugar and mix with a balloon whisk, without overworking, then add the cream, still whisking just lightly. Add the flour and mix with a whisk for 30 seconds. Scrape the vanilla seeds from the pod into the mixture, then add the almonds and use a wooden spoon to mix them in. Cover with cling film and set aside to rest for 20 minutes.

Preheat the oven to 180°C/Gas 4. You will find it easier to bake and shape the tuiles in 2 or 3 batches. Generously butter a large baking sheet. Stir the tuile mixture with a wooden spoon, then use a soup spoon to drop little mounds of mixture in staggered rows onto the baking sheet, spacing 8cm apart, to allow plenty of room for spreading. Press each mound lightly with a fork. Bake for 10 minutes, until pale golden brown.

As soon as they come out of the oven, slide a palette knife under a tuile and place in a tuile mould, or drape it over a rolling pin. Repeat for all the tuiles, working rapidly before they cool down on the baking sheet and become too brittle to mould. If any have hardened, put back in the oven for 30 seconds to soften enough to be shaped.

Once all the tuiles have cooled in the mould or over the rolling pin, carefully remove them to a wire rack. Repeat to bake and shape the rest.

Serve the tuiles dusted with a little icing sugar.

The quality of many of your desserts will depend on the success of these key elements. Creams, or crèmes, are used to fill cakes, crêpes, mille-feuilles etc. Crème patissière plays an essential role in the preparation of soufflés; pastry is used for pies, tarts and tartlets; and my elegant, pillowy sponge fingers are perfect for lining charlottes and bavarois, as well as serving as an accompaniment to creamy mousses and ice creams. And you will find that my three signature sauces – chocolate, orange and caramel – are served with, or suggested as an accompaniment to quite a few of my desserts.

basics

crème chantilly

makes about 600g

500ml whipping cream, well chilled
50g icing sugar or 50ml stock syrup (page 275)
1 vanilla pod, split lengthways

Put the chilled cream and icing sugar or stock syrup into the chilled bowl of an electric mixer. Using the tip of a knife, scrape out the seeds from the vanilla pod and add them to the bowl. Beat at medium speed for 1–2 minutes. Increase the speed and beat for another 3–4 minutes, until the cream starts to thicken to a light ribbon consistency; don't overbeat it. (You may, of course, prefer to use a hand whisk.)

Chantilly cream is best used as soon as you have made it, but it will keep in a covered bowl in the fridge for up to 24 hours.

chocolate crème chantilly
Melt 150g good-quality dark chocolate in a bain-marie, taking care not to heat it above 45°C. Stir until smooth and leave to cool slightly, then fold into the crème chantilly.

coffee crème chantilly
Dissolve 2 tbsp instant coffee in 2 tbsp tepid sugar syrup (or use 1 tbsp liquid coffee extract) and add it to the cream before beating it.

frangipane (almond cream)

makes about 500g

125g icing sugar
125g ground almonds
125g butter, at room temperature
25g plain flour, sifted
2 large eggs
25ml rum (optional)

Sift the icing sugar and ground almonds together and set aside. In a large bowl, work the butter with a whisk until creamy. Still whisking, add the icing sugar and almond mixture, then the flour. When the mixture is evenly combined, incorporate the eggs one by one, whisking between each addition. You should now have a smooth, light cream. Stir in the rum if you wish.

This cream will keep in an airtight container or bowl, covered with cling film, in the fridge for up to a week. Leave it at room temperature for 30 minutes before using.

crème patissière

makes about 750g

6 egg yolks
125g caster sugar
40g plain flour, sifted
500ml milk
1 vanilla pod, split lengthways
a little icing sugar or butter

Whisk the egg yolks and one-third of the sugar together in a bowl to a light ribbon consistency. Whisk in the flour thoroughly.

In a saucepan, heat the milk with the rest of the sugar and the vanilla pod. As soon as it comes to the boil, pour it onto the egg yolk mixture, stirring as you go. Mix well, then return the mixture to the pan. Bring to the boil over a medium heat, stirring continuously with the whisk. Let bubble for 2 minutes, then strain into a bowl.

Dust the crème patissière with a veil of icing sugar to prevent a skin forming as it cools, or dot small flakes of butter all over the surface. Once cold, it can be kept in the fridge for up to 3 days. Remove the vanilla pod before using.

chocolate crème patissière Add 75g melted good-quality dark chocolate to the crème patissière before cooling.

orange butter sauce

serves 6

juice of 6 oranges, about 250g each
100g icing sugar, sifted
125g butter, cut into pieces, softened

Strain the orange juice through a fine sieve or chinois into a heavy-based saucepan and add the icing sugar. Slowly bring to the boil and let bubble over a medium heat until reduced by half.

Turn off the heat and whisk in the softened butter, a little at a time. Serve the sauce at room temperature.

variation A few drops of Grand Marnier or Curaçao can be added for extra warmth.

chocolate sauce

serves 6

200g good-quality dark bitter chocolate,
   70% cocoa solids (preferably Valrhona)
175ml milk
2 tbsp double cream
30g caster sugar
30g butter, diced

Chop the chocolate and place in a heatproof bowl. Set over a pan of gently simmering water and allow to melt slowly, stirring occasionally until very smooth. Take off the heat.

Combine the milk, cream and sugar in a saucepan, stir with a whisk and bring to the boil.

Still stirring with the whisk, pour the boiling milk mixture on to the melted chocolate, then return the mixture to the pan and let it bubble over the heat for a few seconds, stirring continuously.

Turn off the heat and whisk in the butter, a little at a time, to give a smooth, homogeneous sauce. Pass it through a fine sieve or chinois. Serve at once or keep warm in a bain-marie until needed.

variation Try adding a dash of Grand Marnier to enhance the sauce, or infuse the creamy milk mixture with a good pinch of crushed cardamom seeds for a light spicy note.

serves 4

50g caster sugar
40g butter, softened
1 vanilla pod, split lengthways
200ml double cream

Combine the sugar and butter in a heavy-based saucepan. Scrape the seeds from the vanilla pod and add them to the pan. Stir over a very low heat with a wooden spoon until the sugar has dissolved. Continue to cook until the mixture turns an attractive caramel colour. Immediately take the pan off the heat and stir in the cream, protecting your hand with a cloth as the mixture may splutter. Mix well to combine.

Return to a medium heat and cook for 5 minutes, stirring continuously with the wooden spoon. The sauce should be perfectly blended, smooth and shiny. Pass it through a fine sieve or chinois and leave to cool.

Serve the sauce once it has cooled, or refrigerate for up to 3 days.

stock syrup

makes about 700ml

400g caster sugar
50g liquid glucose

Combine the sugar, liquid glucose and 350ml water in a saucepan and bring slowly to the boil over a low heat, stirring continuously with a wooden spoon to dissolve the sugar. Boil for 3 minutes, skimming the surface if necessary.

Pass the syrup through a fine sieve or chinois into a bowl and leave to cool. It will keep in an airtight container in the fridge for up to 2 weeks.

NOTE This basic, light sugar syrup is used to make fruit coulis, sorbets etc. For a heavy stock syrup, to use in a rich sauce for example, boil the syrup further until reduced by one-third.

joconde sponge

makes a 40x60cm thin sponge

185g icing sugar
185g ground almonds
5 eggs, plus 5 egg whites
25g caster sugar
40g butter, melted and cooled
50g plain flour, sifted

Preheat the oven to 200°C/Gas 6 and line a 40x60cm baking sheet with non-stick baking parchment or a silicone liner.

Sift the icing sugar and ground almonds together into a bowl, add the whole eggs and whisk to a ribbon consistency. In a separate bowl, whisk the egg whites to soft peaks, then whisk in the caster sugar until the mixture holds firm peaks.

Carefully fold the cooled, melted butter into the whole egg mixture, followed by the flour. Now gently mix in one-third of the whisked whites until evenly combined, then delicately fold in the rest of the whites, taking care not to overwork the mixture.

Using a palette knife, spread the mixture smoothly over the lined baking sheet to a thickness of 3–5mm. Immediately bake for 2–3 minutes, until the sponge is just firm to the touch. Slide the sponge on its paper (or liner) onto a wire rack and leave to cool.

Once cooled, cut out rounds or other shapes, using a metal cutter, to use as a base for serving mousses and other desserts. If only half the quantity is needed, freeze the rest, well wrapped, for another dessert.

makes a 40x60cm thin sponge

60g very finely ground almonds
180g very finely ground hazelnuts
250g icing sugar, sifted
110g plain flour, sifted
150ml egg whites (about 5 medium)
100g caster sugar

Preheat the oven to 180°C/Gas 4 and line a 40x60cm baking sheet with non-stick baking parchment or a silicone liner.

In a bowl, thoroughly mix the ground almonds and hazelnuts with the icing sugar and flour. In another large bowl, whisk the egg whites to soft peaks, then whisk in the caster sugar until the mixture holds firm peaks. Sift the ground nut mix onto the egg whites, then delicately fold in, using a large slotted spoon, taking care not to overwork the mixture.

Using a palette knife, spread the mixture smoothly over the lined baking sheet to a thickness of about 7mm. Immediately bake for 12–15 minutes, until the sponge is just firm to the touch but still slightly soft in the middle. Slide the sponge on its paper (or liner) onto a wire rack and leave to cool.

Once cooled, cut out rounds or other shapes, using a metal cutter, to use as a base for parfaits, mousses and other desserts. If only half the quantity is needed, freeze the rest, well wrapped, for another dessert.

brioche dough

makes about 1.2kg dough

70ml tepid milk
15g fresh yeast
500g plain flour
1 tbsp fine salt
6 eggs
350g butter, slightly softened, plus extra to grease
30g caster sugar
1 egg yolk mixed with 1 tbsp milk (eggwash)

Put the milk and yeast into a bowl and stir to dissolve the yeast. Put the flour, salt and eggs into an electric mixer fitted with a dough hook and pour in the milk and yeast mixture. Mix on low speed to combine and knead the dough for 5 minutes.

Scrape down the sides of the bowl with a rubber spatula, then knead at medium speed for about 10 minutes. By this stage, the dough should be smooth, elastic and well amalgamated.

Meanwhile, in another bowl, mix the butter and sugar together well. Add a few small pieces to the dough, then with the mixer running at low speed, add the rest, a piece a time. When the butter mixture is all incorporated, increase the speed and work for 6–10 minutes, until the dough is very smooth and shiny, and comes away from the bowl with perfect elasticity.

Remove the dough hook, leaving the dough in the bowl. Cover with a tea towel or cling film and leave to rise at approximately 24°C for about 2 hours, until the dough has doubled in volume.

Knock the dough back by flipping it over 2 or 3 times with your hand. Cover the bowl again and refrigerate for several hours (but not more than 24 hours). The dough is then ready to use and mould.

to shape a large brioche
Divide 600g dough into two-thirds (400g) and one-third (200g). Shape the larger piece into a ball and place it in the bottom of a buttered brioche mould, measuring 16cm across the top, 8cm across the base. Make a deep indentation. Shape the small piece of dough into an elongated oval and gently press into the indentation in the large ball, so that only a little is left visible, resembling a 'head'. Lightly brush the dough with eggwash. Leave to rise at approximately 24°C for about 1¹/₂ hours, until it has at least doubled in volume. Preheat the oven to 200°C/Gas 6. Brush the brioche lightly again with eggwash. Bake for 15 minutes, then lower the setting to 170°C/Gas 3 and bake for another 30 minutes. Leave the brioche in the mould for 5 minutes, then unmould onto a wire rack and leave to cool.

NOTE This classic French dough can be frozen, well wrapped, for up to 2 weeks. To use, leave to thaw in the fridge for 12 hours before moulding it into the required shape and size.

4 eggs, separated, plus 3 egg yolks
85g caster sugar
35g plain flour
40g potato flour
about 100g icing sugar, sifted

Preheat the oven to 220°C/Gas 7 and line a 40x60cm baking sheet with a silicone liner.

In a bowl, whisk the 7 egg yolks with two-thirds of the caster sugar until you have a ribbon consistency. In a separate bowl, whisk the egg whites to soft peaks, then whisk in the remaining caster sugar until the mixture holds firm peaks.

Carefully fold one-third of the whisked whites into the yolks until evenly combined, then gently fold in the rest of the whisked whites, taking care not to overwork it. Sift the two flours together over the mixture and gently fold in, stopping stirring as soon as the mixture becomes smooth.

Put the mixture into a piping bag fitted with a plain nozzle, about 1cm. Pipe the mixture into 8cm lengths, either straight or on the diagonal, leaving a 2cm space between each to make sure that they don't touch each other. Immediately sprinkle icing sugar generously over the top and leave at room temperature for 5 minutes.

Give a second, lighter dusting (this will create a pearly beading effect on cooking). Bake for 6–8 minutes, until pale golden. Leave on the silicone liner for 1 minute, then carefully lift off with a palette knife and place on a wire rack to cool.

Stored in a sealed container, these sponge fingers keep very well for up to a week.

sponge bases
Spread (rather than pipe) the mixture smoothly with a palette knife onto the silicone liner to cover evenly, then bake as above. Once cooled, cut out little rounds, using a metal cutter, to use as a base for serving ice creams or sorbets.

makes about 650g

250g plain flour, sifted
200g butter, cut into small pieces,
   slightly softened

100g icing sugar, sifted
pinch of salt
2 egg yolks

Heap the flour in a mound on the work surface and make a well. Put in the butter, icing sugar and salt. With your fingertips, mix and cream the butter with the sugar and salt, then add the egg yolks and work them in delicately with your fingertips. Little by little, draw the flour into the centre and work the mixture delicately with your fingers until you have a homogeneous dough.

Using the palm of your hand, push the dough away from you 3 or 4 times until it is completely smooth. Roll it into a ball, wrap in cling film and refrigerate until ready to use.

If well wrapped, this delicate, sweet pastry will keep in the fridge for up to a week, or in the freezer for up to 3 months.

rough puff pastry

makes 1.2kg

500g plain flour
500g very cold butter, cut into small cubes
1 tsp salt
250ml ice-cold water

Heap the flour in a mound on the work surface and make a well. Put in the butter and salt and work them together with the fingertips of one hand, gradually drawing the flour into the centre with the other hand.

When the cubes of butter have become small pieces and the dough is grainy, gradually add the iced water and mix until it is all incorporated, but don't overwork the dough. Roll it into a ball, wrap in cling film and refrigerate for 20 minutes.

Flour the work surface and roll out the pastry to a 40x20cm rectangle. Fold it into three and give it a quarter-turn. Roll the block of pastry into a 40x20cm rectangle as before, and fold it into three again. These are the first 2 turns. Wrap the block in cling film and refrigerate it for 30 minutes.

Give the chilled pastry another 2 turns, rolling and folding as before. This makes a total of 4 turns, and the pastry is now ready. Wrap it in cling film and refrigerate for at least 30 minutes before using.

Tightly wrapped in cling film, this quick puff pastry will keep for 3 days in the fridge, and for at least 4 weeks in the freezer.

Bain-marie This is literally a water bath, used to control the cooking of delicate custards etc., and to keep delicate sauces warm. A bowl over a pan of simmering or hot water functions as a bain-marie on the hob; in the oven a baking dish may be placed in a roasting pan containing hot water.

Bake blind To bake an empty pastry case, either partially or fully, before adding the filling. Line the pastry case with greaseproof paper and fill with ceramic baking beans or dried pulses before baking. The beans and paper are then removed and the tart returned to the oven to dry the base (or cook it fully if the filling isn't to be baked in the case).

Blanch To plunge an ingredient briefly into boiling water, usually for 30–60 seconds, then refresh in cold water to loosen the skin (of peaches, for example) or par-cook.

Butter To brush a mould or baking sheet with melted or softened butter.

Butter, clarified To prepare, melt butter very gently in a saucepan and then bring it to the boil. Ladle the clear butter through a muslin-lined sieve, leaving the milky deposit in the bottom of the pan.

Caramelise To heat sugar until it dissolves and forms a caramel. Also used to describe cooking foods until their natural sugars – or an applied sugar topping – has browned.

Cartouche A circle of greaseproof paper or baking parchment with a small steam hole cut in the centre laid over the surface of fruit in a poaching liquid (or similar), to keep it immersed and lessen evaporation. To make a cartouche, fold the paper circle into segments, snip off the point and open out. (Illustrated left)

Chinois A conical strainer used for sieving a mixture to make it smooth.

Coulis A thin purée, usually of fruit mixed with a little sugar syrup, of a pourable consistency.

Crimp To pinch up the pastry border of a tart attractively with a pastry crimper or between your index finger and thumb.

Eggwash An egg yolk lightly beaten with 1 tbsp milk, used to lightly brush pastry dough before baking.

Fold in To gently combine one mixture with another, using a rubber spatula or large metal spoon to cut through and turn the mixtures lightly and gently so they are combined with minimum loss of air and lightness.

Glaze To brush or dust the surface of pastry, filling (or other food) with a mixture for colour and shine. Eggwash is often used as a glaze. Icing sugar is sometimes sprinkled over puff pastry, then caramelised in a very hot oven to form the glaze.

Infuse To flavour a liquid, such as a sugar syrup for poaching fruit, or milk for a custard, by immersing aromatics – herbs, spices or vanilla pods, for example – to impart a subtle flavour and aroma. The liquid is usually gently warmed with the flavourings to just below the boil and left to stand for a while before straining out the flavouring ingredients.

Julienne Very fine strips – usually of citrus zest, but also used to describe finely shredded herbs.

Knock back To return a risen yeasted dough to its original volume by lifting it with your lightly floured hand and quickly flipping it over 2 or 3 times.

Macerate To steep fruits in a syrup, sometimes flavoured with alcohol to soften them.

Reduce To boil a liquor steadily to reduce and thicken it by evaporating some of the water.

Refresh To immerse food in cold water immediately after blanching or cooking to stop the cooking process, in order to preserve the colour and texture of the food.

Ribbon consistency Used to describe the texture of whisked cream or a whisked sponge mixture, when it is thick enough to leave a ribbon trail as the beaters are lifted from the bowl.

Toasting (or roasting) nuts Scatter the nuts on a baking tray and place in the oven at 180°C/Gas 4 for 10 minutes, or until evenly coloured, shaking occasionally.

Zest To pare orange, lemon or lime zest with a citrus zester very thinly, leaving behind all the bitter white pith.

acknowledgements

I would like to thank the following people, who have all taken part in the making of this book:
Richard Guérin, a young, highly talented *chef pâtissier*, **Douglas Gregory**, *chef tourier*, and **Michael Nizzero**, *sous-chef*, who all helped me in the preparation of the desserts for the photography.
Martin Brigdale, who yet again leaves me full of wonder at the superb quality of his photographs, and the way they make you want to try my recipes.
Mary Evans, a true *artiste*, who knows how best to advise and guide me in order to get the very best out of me.

Janet Illsley, who calmly and expertly coordinated this work, steering it through its various stages of creation.
Sally Somers, for translating my French text into English with speed, precision and panache.
Claude Grant for typing and editing my French manuscript with her usual proficiency.
Robyn Roux my wife, who kindly checked the English version of my recipes and introductory texts with exemplary patience, for her constant support.

Equipment
In order to achieve the best results, I have opted for the following brands:
For electric mixers – Krupps
For non-stick moulds, tart tins and frying pans – Tefal
For saucepans – All Clad, which allow you to cook crèmes, syrups, caramels etc. to perfection.

For my product of choice *par excellence*, chocolate, I only ever use Valrhona; the quality of their couvertures is unrivalled.